I0065442

A Beginner's Guide to Cryptocurrency and Crypto Investing

How Anyone Can Unlock Wealth and Quickly Master Digital Trading Without Fear of Scams or Complexity

George Munson

GL Digital Publishing LLC

Copyright © 2025 by George Munson

All rights reserved.

No portion of this book may be reproduced in any form without written permission from the publisher or author, except as permitted by U.S. copyright law.

This publication is designed to provide accurate and authoritative information regarding the subject matter covered. It is sold with the understanding that neither the author nor the publisher is engaged in rendering legal, investment, accounting, or other professional services.

While the publisher and author have used their best efforts in preparing this book, they make no representations or warranties with respect to the accuracy or completeness of the contents of this book and specifically disclaim any implied warranties of merchantability or fitness for a particular purpose. No warranty may be created or extended by sales representatives or written sales materials.

The advice and strategies contained herein may not be suitable for your situation. You should consult with a professional when appropriate. Neither the publisher nor the author shall be liable for any loss of profit or any other commercial damages, including but not limited to special, incidental, consequential, personal, or other damages.

Neither the publisher nor the author claim responsibility for the persistence or accuracy of URLs for external or third-party Internet Websites referred to in this publication and does not guarantee that any content on such Websites is, or will remain, accurate or appropriate.

Designations used by companies to distinguish their products are often claimed as trademarks. All brand names and product names used in this book and on its cover are trade names, service marks, trademarks, and registered trademarks of their respective owners. The publishers and the book are not associated with any product or vendor mentioned in this book. None of the companies referenced within the book have endorsed the book.

First Edition 2025

To all my friends and family who asked so many questions...
I had to write a book!
With Love

Contents

Introduction

In a bustling café in Tokyo, a young entrepreneur, let's call her Aiko, sits across from her business partner. They're discussing a groundbreaking project that could reshape their industry. Aiko, who is based in Tokyo, needs to make a business deal with her partner, who is in New York. Instead of cash, they exchange cryptocurrency, finalizing the deal with a few taps on their smartphones. This simple act highlights the transformative power of digital currencies—bridging distances and breaking down financial barriers. Such is the potential of cryptocurrency, a revolution in the making.

Cryptocurrency has come a long way since Bitcoin emerged in 2009. This digital currency, created by an unknown person using Satoshi Nakamoto's pseudonym, introduced the world to blockchain technology. Over the years, Bitcoin and other cryptocurrencies have captured the imagination of millions, promising a decentralized financial system. Unlike traditional banks, this system is not controlled by any single entity, making it more transparent and resistant to manipulation. Today, cryptocurrency is not just a buzzword but a pivotal part of the global economic landscape.

This book serves as a practical guide for those new to cryptocurrency. It breaks down complex concepts into digestible information, offering actionable advice for navigating this new financial frontier. Here, you'll find the answers to questions about buying, trading, and safeguarding your digital assets. I aim to provide clarity and simplicity, ensuring you can confidently engage with cryptocurrency.

My vision is straightforward: to demystify cryptocurrency and empower you to embrace this innovation. I understand the intimidation of venturing into unknown territory, especially as dynamic as digital currencies. This book aims to cut through the noise, focusing on what truly matters: understanding the basics and making informed decisions.

My readers range in age from young adults to seniors. Whether you're a curious beginner or looking to diversify your financial portfolio, this book is for you. You may be motivated by the potential for economic growth, the allure of new technology, or the desire to understand an emerging market. I designed the content to meet your needs and address any challenges you might face, such as understanding the technical jargon, navigating the volatile market, or ensuring the security of your digital assets.

The book is structured to guide you through essential topics. It begins with the basics of cryptocurrency and blockchain technology. From there, we explore trading strategies, securing digital assets, and recognizing scams. Each chapter builds on the last, providing a roadmap that takes you from novice to knowledgeable participant in the crypto space.

Why is this book important now? The cryptocurrency market is evolving rapidly, influencing global finance in unprecedented ways. As more institutions and individuals adopt digital currencies, understanding them becomes crucial. This book offers a timely exploration of these developments, equipping you with the knowledge to stay ahead.

On a personal note, I am passionate about helping others understand cryptocurrency. It has the potential to drive financial growth and independence. I am motivated to write this book to provide reliable, easy-to-follow guidance. I am committed to supporting you on this journey and ensuring you navigate the crypto space confidently, feeling empowered by your understanding.

To get the most out of this book, actively engage with its content. Apply the strategies and insights to your financial journey. Embrace cryptocurrency's opportunities and feel committed to exploring this exciting landscape.

As we close this introduction, consider the future of cryptocurrency. It holds the potential for immense wealth creation and financial independence. The opportunities are vast, and the journey is just beginning. Let this book be your guide as you step into the world of digital currencies, ready to seize the possibilities that lie ahead.

Chapter One

Understanding the Basics of Cryptocurrency

A few years ago, a young developer in Berlin decided to pay for his lunch using Bitcoin. The transaction cost him a fraction of a cent and registered before he finished his coffee. This simple act encapsulated a new era of financial interaction—one where speed, efficiency, and decentralization came to the fore. Cryptocurrency, initially a niche interest, has become a significant force reshaping how we think about money. This chapter will lay the foundation for understanding what cryptocurrency is, its purpose, and why it matters in today's world.

What is Cryptocurrency?

Cryptocurrency is a form of digital money that uses cryptographic techniques to secure transactions. Unlike traditional currency, it exists solely in digital form and is not backed by any physical commodity. Imagine a version of cash that you can use online, entirely free from the control of banks or governments. This is cryptocurrency—a decentralized currency that operates on blockchain technology, making it secure and transparent.

The idea behind cryptocurrency is to create a financial system that transcends borders and provides financial services to everyone, regardless of geographic location. At its core, cryptocurrency aims to solve two major issues: financial inclusivity and high transaction costs. Cryptocurrencies allow direct peer-to-peer transactions by eliminating intermediaries, lowering costs, and accelerating processes. For many, this means access to financial tools that were previously unreachable, democratizing the economic landscape.

Traditional currencies, known as fiat money, are issued and regulated by central authorities like governments and banks. They hold physical forms, such as coins and banknotes, and derive their value from the trust people place in the issuing authority. Conversely, cryptocurrencies are decentralized, meaning they have no central authority or government backing. They only exist digitally and are governed by a computer network that validates and records transactions. This lack of physical presence and centralization sets cryptocurrencies apart from fiat money.

A key feature of many cryptocurrencies is their digital scarcity. Take Bitcoin, for instance. It has a maximum supply of 21 million coins, a limit coded into its protocol to prevent inflation. This scarcity introduces a new economic model, contrasting sharply with the fiat system, where central banks can print money as needed, often leading to inflation. This limited supply creates value and rarity akin to precious metals like gold. It also introduces an element of economic stability, as the supply is predictable and immune to the whims of governmental monetary policy.

Think About Your Financial Goals

- Consider how cryptocurrency's unique features might align with your financial goals.

- Are you seeking a more inclusive financial system, or are you interested in low-cost transactions?

- Do you value the idea of digital scarcity?

Take a moment to reflect on these questions and jot down your thoughts. This reflection will help frame your understanding as you further explore the world of cryptocurrency.

Decoding the Blockchain: The Backbone of Crypto

Imagine an enormous public ledger that records every transaction ever made, yet no single entity controls it. This type of ledger is blockchain technology—a distributed ledger system that underpins every cryptocurrency. Unlike traditional databases managed by a central authority, blockchains operate on networks of computers, each holding a copy of the entire ledger. This decentralization is key to its security and transparency. Each transaction is grouped into a block, and once the block is filled, it links to the previous one, forming a chronological chain. This structure ensures that once data is added, it becomes nearly impossible to alter without altering subsequent blocks, thus preserving the integrity of the entire chain.

The blockchain achieves its security through cryptographic hashing, which converts transaction data into a fixed-size string of characters, creating a unique digital fingerprint for each block. Any change to the data alters the hash, immediately alerting the network to potential tampering. This hashing, combined with the consensus mechanisms that require the majority of network nodes to agree on the validity of transactions, makes the blockchain extremely robust. The immutable record maintained by blockchain adds another layer of security, building trust among users by ensuring that every transaction is transparent and verifiable.

Beyond its role in cryptocurrencies, blockchain technology holds immense potential in various fields. It enhances supply chain management by providing a real-time ledger of product movements, ensuring authenticity and reducing fraud. For instance, a coffee company can trace the beans from farm to cup, verifying their origin and quality. Smart contracts, another innovative application, are self-executing contracts with the terms of the agreement directly written into code. These can automate complex processes like mortgage approvals, eliminating intermediaries and reducing the risk of human error. The versatility and security of blockchain make it a revolutionary tool, and as technology evolves, overcoming its challenges will be crucial for its continued growth and integration into everyday life.

While the potential of blockchain is vast, it faces challenges that cannot be ignored. Scalability is a significant hurdle, as the current infrastructure struggles to quickly handle large volumes of transactions. This issue is analogous to a highway designed for fewer cars, which leads to congestion as traffic increases. Moreover, the energy consumption of blockchain, particularly in networks like Bitcoin, is a growing concern. The computational power required for mining—the process of validating and recording transactions—is immense, leading to a high carbon footprint. Balancing the benefits of blockchain with its environmental impact remains a critical discussion among developers and policymakers. Understanding these challenges is essential for anyone interested in cryptocurrency, as it provides a realistic view of the technology's current state.

Blockchain's versatility and security make it a revolutionary tool. As technology evolves, overcoming these challenges will be crucial for its continued growth and integration into everyday life. Understanding blockchain is essential for anyone interested in cryptocurrency, as it is the backbone of this digital revolution.

A Glossary of Crypto Terms Made Easy

Understanding the language is key in the vibrant and often bewildering cryptocurrency world. Let's begin with HODL, a term from a misspelled forum post that has since become a rallying cry for crypto enthusiasts. It stands for 'Hold On for Dear Life' and advises investors to keep their assets during market downturns rather than sell in panic. Imagine a stormy sea where seasoned sailors hold tight, trusting the waves will calm. That's HODL in action—weathering the storm of market volatility with the belief that brighter days are ahead. This term, born out of a typo, has become a symbol of resilience and community in the cryptocurrency world, connecting investors in their shared belief in the future of digital currencies.

Next, we encounter the enigmatic whale. In the crypto ocean, whales are investors who hold significant amounts of cryptocurrency. These investors can sway market prices with their trades like a whale influencing the surrounding currents. Imagine a bustling market suddenly slowing because a large buyer enters—this is what happens when a whale makes a move. Their actions are watched closely, as they can cause significant ripples across the trading landscape.

Decentralized Finance, or DeFi, represents a shift from traditional financial systems to a model without intermediaries. DeFi platforms offer services like lending, borrowing, and trading directly through smart contracts on the blockchain. Imagine lending your assets to someone across the globe without ever stepping into a bank. That's DeFi—financial services reimagined for the digital age, offering accessibility and control to users worldwide.

Non-fungible tokens, or NFTs, much like a certificate of ownership, are unique digital assets representing ownership of specific items like art, music, or collectibles. Unlike cryptocurrencies such as Bitcoin, each NFT is distinct and cannot be exchanged as equals. Consider owning a rare baseball card that has no identical counterpart. You wouldn't trade it for just any other baseball card. NFTs operate similarly, with each token holding individual value and significance, often verified through blockchain technology.

Initial Coin Offerings, or ICOs, are a method for new crypto projects to raise funds by selling tokens to early investors. They are akin to crowdfunding but within the crypto realm. Think of a startup selling shares to gather capital, but they offer digital tokens instead of stocks. ICOs can be lucrative but risky, as the market has opportunities and pitfalls.

Newcomers often confuse the distinction between coins and tokens. Coins operate on their blockchains, like Bitcoin and Ethereum. On the other hand, Tokens are built on existing blockchains and often serve specific purposes within platforms. Imagine a theme park where coins are the general currency and tokens are special ride tickets. Both have value, but their roles differ fundamentally.

Another cornerstone concept is decentralization, which refers to the distribution of control across a network rather than a single entity. It promises security and autonomy, as no single point of failure exists. Picture a sprawling city with no central government, where each neighborhood self-governs. This structure mirrors the decentralized nature of cryptocurrencies and their networks.

A visual aid like a flowchart can simplify these terms. Imagine a diagram illustrating blockchain transactions, from initiation to validation, alongside a chart showing market capitalization trends. Visual tools can demystify these complex ideas, providing clarity and reinforcing understanding. By learning this vocabulary, you gain the keys to unlock the intricacies of cryptocurrency, preparing you for deeper comprehension.

Beyond Bitcoin are Altcoins and Tokens

The cryptocurrency landscape extends far beyond the pioneering Bitcoin, introducing many digital assets known as altcoins. Altcoins, short for alternative coins, encompass any digital currency other than Bitcoin. They vary significantly in purpose and technology. Ethereum stands out as a prime example, renowned for its versatility and robust platform that supports a vast range of applications. Unlike Bitcoin, which primarily serves as a digital currency, Ethereum enables developers to build decentralized applications (dApps) using its smart contract functionality. This feature allows automatic transactions when certain conditions are met, offering a foundation for industry innovations from finance to gaming.

Another type of digital asset is tokens, which often operate on existing blockchains like Ethereum. Tokens can be divided into two main categories: utility and security tokens. Utility tokens provide users access to a product or service within a particular platform, like a key granting entry to a digital ecosystem. They are crucial for functionalities within decentralized applications, such as granting voting rights or access to premium features. Security tokens represent ownership in an asset or organization, akin to traditional securities like stocks. These tokens are subject to regulatory oversight, offering investors a stake in the underlying asset or company.

Altcoins and tokens play diverse roles in the crypto ecosystem, each contributing unique functionalities. On Ethereum, smart contracts automate processes that traditionally require intermediaries, significantly reducing costs and increasing efficiency. This ability spurred the growth of decentralized finance (DeFi). This sector enables users to lend, borrow, and trade assets without relying on traditional banks. DeFi platforms use smart contracts to facilitate these transactions, giving users unprecedented control over their financial activities.

The diversity of crypto assets is vast, encompassing privacy coins like Monero, which prioritize transaction anonymity, and stablecoins like Tether, which offer price stability by pegging their value to a fiat currency. These assets cater to different user needs, from those seeking enhanced privacy to those desiring stability in volatile markets.

However, investing in altcoins carries both risks and rewards. Their volatility can lead to significant market speculation, with prices subject to dramatic swings. Investors may experience substantial gains or losses in short periods, making it crucial to approach altcoin investments cautiously. On the upside, altcoins often drive technological innovation, introducing new features and solutions that push the boundaries of the cryptocurrency space. They attract developers and entrepreneurs eager to explore untapped potential, fostering an environment ripe for creativity and advancement.

Wallets 101: Safeguarding Your Digital Coins

The world of cryptocurrency hinges on one fundamental aspect: security. The crypto wallet is at the heart of this security, a digital tool essential for storing, sending, and receiving digital currencies. In essence, a wallet acts like your personal vault in the cryptocurrency realm. There are various types of wallets, each with its features and levels of security. Hot wallets are connected to the internet, offering convenience for frequent transactions. They reside on your smartphone or computer, making them as accessible as your email. However, this accessibility comes at a cost—vulnerability to online threats.

In contrast, cold wallets are offline, akin to a safe deposit box for digital assets. These include hardware wallets like ledgers, which store private keys on a physical device, disconnected from the web, thus shielding them from hackers. For those who prioritize security, cold wallets are often the preferred choice.

When selecting a wallet, security should be your foremost concern. Your wallet's private key is the linchpin of this security. It functions like a password, granting access to your funds, and must remain confidential. If someone else gains control of it, they gain control of your cryptocurrency.

To bolster security, enable two-factor authentication wherever possible. Doing so adds an extra layer of protection, requiring a second verification form—like a code sent to your phone—before access is granted. Think of it as adding a deadbolt to your front door. This simple step can thwart unauthorized access and give you peace of mind.

Setting up a crypto wallet is straightforward. Take Coinbase, for instance. Begin by downloading the app or visiting their website. Create an account using your email and a strong password, then verify your identity through their KYC (Know Your Customer) process, which involves uploading identification documents. Once verified, navigate to the wallet section and follow the prompts to create a new wallet. It's crucial to securely store your recovery phrase, a sequence of words that can restore your wallet if you lose access. This phrase is your lifeline, so treat it with the utmost care. Please write it down, store it safely, and never share it online.

Maintaining the security of your wallet is an ongoing task. Regularly updating your software ensures you have the latest security patches and features. This practice protects against vulnerabilities and keeps your wallet robust. Additionally, avoid using public Wi-Fi networks for transactions. These networks are often unsecured, providing an ideal environment for cybercriminals to intercept data. Instead, make your transactions over a secure, private internet connection. If you must use public Wi-Fi, consider employing a Virtual Private Network (VPN) to encrypt and shield your data from prying eyes.

Ensuring the security of your digital coins is not just about choosing the right wallet; it's about vigilance and responsible management. By adopting these security practices, you safeguard your assets against potential threats. The world of cryptocurrency offers exciting possibilities, but the responsibility of protecting your investments comes with it. Understanding these wallet fundamentals is crucial to confidently navigating the crypto landscape.

The Role of Exchanges in Cryptocurrency Trading

You are walking into a bustling marketplace, where traders shout prices and deals are struck with a handshake. In the digital age, cryptocurrency exchanges play a similar role. Digital currency markets are platforms for buying, selling, and trading various cryptocurrencies. Think of them as the grand bazaars of the digital world. At the heart of these exchanges lies the order book system, which matches buy and sell orders based on price and volume. When a buyer is willing to purchase at a seller's price, a match occurs, and the transaction is executed. This system enables efficient trading, ensuring liquidity and price discovery in the market. Market makers, often sophisticated traders or algorithms, provide liquidity by placing buy and sell orders, ensuring enough activity to facilitate trades. They bridge gaps between buyers and sellers, stabilizing prices and reducing volatility, much like seasoned merchants who provide a steady supply of goods.

Exchanges primarily come in two forms: centralized and decentralized. Centralized exchanges, like Binance, operate with an intermediary that facilitates trades and holds user assets. These platforms often offer a user-friendly interface, high liquidity, and a broad range of cryptocurrencies. However, they require users to trust the platform with their funds, a factor that can be both a comfort and a risk. On the other hand, decentralized exchanges like Uniswap allow direct peer-to-peer transactions without intermediaries. They run on smart contracts, offering users greater control over their funds and enhanced privacy. Yet, this comes with challenges like lower liquidity and a more complex user experience akin to navigating a self-service store without a guide.

Choosing the proper exchange can feel like picking the appropriate marketplace. Security should top your list of considerations. Look for exchanges with robust security features. These exchanges include two-factor authentication and cold storage for funds. The range of available cryptocurrencies is another factor—ensure the platform supports the assets you wish to trade. Additionally, consider the exchange's reputation, fees, and user experience. A platform with a strong track record and positive user reviews can provide peace of mind, much like a trusted local market.

Despite their advantages, exchanges carry inherent risks. Exchange hacks remain a significant threat, with cybercriminals targeting platforms that hold large sums of digital currencies. To mitigate this risk, consider transferring your funds to a secure wallet rather than leaving them on the exchange. Regulatory compliance is another critical aspect. Different jurisdictions impose varying regulations on exchanges, affecting their operations and your access to services. Choosing exchanges that comply with relevant laws and ensuring your investments are protected under legal frameworks are crucial. Navigating the world of cryptocurrency exchanges requires diligence and informed decision-making. Like choosing a trusted vendor in a crowded market, selecting the proper exchange involves balancing convenience, security, and personal preferences to ensure a safe and seamless trading experience.

Understanding the Differences Between Fiat vs. Crypto

Fiat currency and cryptocurrency are two distinct yet interwoven entities in finance. Fiat money, like the dollar or euro, is government-issued and controlled by central banks, serving as the backbone of the global economy. It's a system of trust where value is derived from the belief in the issuing authority. In contrast, cryptocurrencies operate on a decentralized network free from governmental control. They rely on a peer-to-peer system where power rests with the user community. This decentralization means no single entity can manipulate the currency, offering its users a sense of autonomy and security.

The dynamics of inflation further differentiate the two. Fiat currencies are susceptible to inflation, as central banks can print more money, diluting value over time. Doing so often leads to decreased purchasing power, affecting savings and investments. Cryptocurrencies like Bitcoin, with their capped supply, present a stark contrast. Their limited availability curbs inflation risks, preserving value over time. However, this doesn't make cryptocurrencies immune to volatility. Their prices can fluctuate wildly, driven by market speculation and demand. It's a double-edged sword, offering a hedge against traditional inflation and the potential for rapid depreciation.

Cryptocurrencies offer clear advantages over fiat in certain areas. For one, they enable rapid international transactions. Transferring money across borders can be cumbersome and costly with fiat, involving bank fees and processing delays. Cryptocurrencies cut through this red tape and directly allow fast, low-cost user transfers. Additionally, they offer enhanced privacy. Transactions are pseudonymous and recorded on a public ledger without revealing personal information. This appeals to those valuing discretion and security, though it also raises concerns about potential misuse by illicit activities.

Yet, cryptocurrencies face significant hurdles in replacing fiat. Scalability remains a challenge as networks struggle to handle a high volume of transactions efficiently. This volume can lead to delays and increased fees during peak times, limiting usability. Moreover, acceptance of cryptocurrencies as a mainstream payment method is limited. While some retailers embrace digital currencies, widespread adoption is still taking place. Many people remain hesitant, unsure about the stability and practicality of using cryptocurrencies for everyday transactions.

Despite these challenges, fiat and cryptocurrencies are not mutually exclusive. They can coexist, each complementing the other's strengths. Hybrid financial systems are emerging, integrating cryptocurrencies into traditional banking frameworks. These systems offer the best of both worlds, providing fiat stability with crypto's innovation. Cryptocurrencies facilitate quick, cost-effective transactions in cross-border transfers, while fiat ensures compliance with local regulations and stability. It's a symbiotic relationship where each serves a purpose, creating a more versatile financial ecosystem.

Understanding the nuances between fiat and cryptocurrencies is crucial in this evolving landscape. Recognizing their unique characteristics and potential co-action can help you navigate the financial world confidently. Whether you're intrigued by crypto's decentralization or comforted by fiat's stability, both play a role in shaping the future of money. As these worlds continue to intertwine, they offer new opportunities and challenges, redefining how we think about value, exchange, and trust.

Chapter Two

Navigating the Cryptocurrency Market

You are standing at the helm of a vast and uncharted sea, with the winds of opportunity and risk swirling around you. The cryptocurrency market is where fortunes can be made or lost in the blink of an eye. Navigating this market requires more than intuition; it demands understanding the tools and techniques seasoned traders use for decisions. Among these, crypto charts are invaluable, offering a window into digital currencies' past, present, and potential future.

Reading crypto charts might initially seem daunting, but grasping the basics is akin to learning a new language that opens doors to hidden insights. At the heart of these charts are candlestick patterns, line graphs, and bar charts, each serving a unique purpose. Candlestick charts are the most popular, with their colorful bodies showing opening, closing, and high and low prices for specific periods. These visualizations originated in 18th-century Japan for rice trading and have since become integral to financial markets worldwide. Line charts, while simpler, provide a clear view of general trends and long-term movements. Bar charts offer similar information to candlesticks but with a more understated presentation.

Understanding these foundational elements is crucial for analyzing trends and determining price movements.

Delving deeper into chart indicators enhances this analysis by offering clues about the market's direction. Moving averages, for instance, smooth out price data, helping traders identify the overall trend. They act like a compass, pointing towards the prevailing direction amidst the market's noise. The Relative Strength Index (RSI), on the other hand, assesses whether an asset is overbought or oversold, signaling potential reversals. Picture a pendulum swinging too far in one direction—RSI helps anticipate when it might swing back. Combined, these indicators provide a more comprehensive picture of the market's health, aiding in making informed decisions.

Spotting trends and patterns in these charts is like reading the ocean's currents, revealing where the market might head next. Trends often manifest through recognizable formations, such as the head and shoulders pattern, which can indicate a reversal. A bullish engulfing pattern, where a larger upward candle follows a smaller downward one, suggests a potential price increase. Conversely, a bearish engulfing pattern warns of a possible downturn. By recognizing these patterns, traders can anticipate movements, like predicting the weather by observing the clouds.

Timeframes are pivotal in chart analysis, offering different perspectives on market trends. Intraday charts, which track hourly or minute-to-minute activity, are ideal for those seeking to capitalize on short-term movements. They provide a high-resolution view, capturing the market's rapid fluctuations. Weekly charts, however, cater to those interested in understanding longer-term trends, smoothing out daily volatility to reveal the market's broader trajectory. Whether you're a day trader or a long-term investor, choosing the right timeframe is akin to selecting the right lens for your binoculars, allowing you to focus on the details that matter most to your strategy.

Enhancing Your Chart Analysis Skills

- Try exploring a charting platform like TradingView.

- Choose a cryptocurrency and apply a moving average and RSI to its chart.

- Observe how these indicators interact with the price movement and note any patterns you recognize.

- Reflect on how these insights might influence your trading decisions.

Understanding crypto charts and their components is not just about mastering the art of navigation. It's about empowering yourself with the tools to confidently steer your investments through the cryptocurrency market's ups and downs. As you continue to explore this dynamic landscape, these skills will prove invaluable in making informed, strategic decisions, giving you a sense of control and confidence in your trading journey.

Identifying Bull and Bear Markets

Again, imagine the cryptocurrency market as a vast ocean, with waves representing the ups and downs of prices. Just like the tides, these movements follow patterns known as bull and bear markets.

A bull market is a sustained upward trend where prices consistently rise, fueled by optimism and confidence. In this scenario, investors eagerly accumulate and diversify their assets, much like collectors at an art auction.

Key indicators of a bull market include increasing trading volume, rising prices across various cryptocurrencies, and widespread media attention.

On the other hand, a bear market reflects a prolonged downward trend. In this case, fear and pessimism dominate, leading to widespread selling. Investors may choose to sell assets or adopt short-selling strategies to profit from declining prices. Understanding these market conditions is crucial for making informed decisions in crypto trading.

The emotional currents driving these markets are powerful. Greed and fear are the primary psychological forces influencing investor behavior. In bull markets, where the fear of missing out (FOMO) can lead to impulsive buying, or bear markets, where fear prompts panic selling, emotions can lead to rapid price swings and market volatility. But remember, emotions, while natural, should not dictate your actions. Instead, use them as indicators to guide your understanding of market sentiment, helping you control your trading decisions.

Market cycles consist of distinct phases that reflect changes in investor behavior. The accumulation phase occurs when informed investors buy assets at lower prices, often after a bear market. This quiet period resembles a gardener planting seeds in preparation for growth. As prices rise, the market enters the markup phase, where momentum builds, and more participants join the buying frenzy. Eventually, the market reaches the distribution phase, where savvy investors sell their assets to less experienced buyers, much like a store clearing out inventory. This phase often precedes a downturn, leading to the markdown phase of a bear market. Here, panic selling intensifies, driving prices down further. Understanding these phases helps you anticipate shifts in market trends and position yourself accordingly.

Using different strategies, you can thrive in varying market conditions. During bear markets, consider dollar-cost averaging. This approach involves investing a fixed amount regularly, regardless of price fluctuations. By spreading your investments over time, you smooth out the effects of volatility, much like sailing with a steady hand through choppy waters. This strategy reduces the impact of market downturns and allows you to accumulate lower-priced assets.

In contrast, bull markets present opportunities for profit-taking. Consider selling a portion of your holdings to lock in gains as prices rise. This approach helps you avoid the pitfalls of greed and ensures you capitalize on favorable market conditions. You can confidently navigate bullish and bearish markets by strategically adjusting your investments.

Recognizing bull and bear markets, understanding the psychological factors, and employing strategic approaches to capitalizing on these conditions equip you to make informed decisions. As you continue to explore the cryptocurrency market, let these insights guide your path, ensuring you remain adaptable and prepared for whatever challenges and opportunities lie ahead.

Understanding Market Capitalization and Volume

Imagine again, we're standing in a bustling marketplace, where the worth of goods fluctuates with each passing moment. You can see this dynamic in the cryptocurrency market through market capitalization and trading volume. Market capitalization, often referred to as market cap, represents the total value of a cryptocurrency. Multiplying the total circulating supply of coins by the current price per coin equals the market cap. This figure provides a snapshot of a cryptocurrency's overall worth, acting like a barometer for its size and influence within the market. High market-cap cryptocurrencies, like Bitcoin and Ethereum, are often seen as stable and established, akin to blue-chip stocks. Meanwhile, smaller market cap coins may offer higher returns but come with increased volatility and risk.

Trading volume, on the other hand, measures the total number of coins traded within a specific timeframe. It indicates market activity and liquidity, revealing how easily a cryptocurrency can be bought or sold without significantly affecting its price. High trading volume suggests a healthy, liquid market where transactions occur swiftly. It can also indicate investor interest and confidence in a cryptocurrency. Conversely, low volume might signal a lack of interest or potential liquidity issues, making it harder to execute large trades without causing price disruptions. Volume spikes can sometimes reveal underlying trends or signal market manipulation, such as pump-and-dump schemes, where prices inflate before a sudden sell-off.

Categorizing cryptocurrencies into large-cap, mid-cap, and small-cap is based on market capitalization. Large-cap cryptocurrencies, like Bitcoin, boast significant market caps and are generally considered more secure investments, though with modest returns compared to their smaller counterparts. Mid-cap cryptocurrencies balance risk and reward, often representing emerging projects with growth potential. With their lower market caps, small-cap cryptocurrencies present opportunities for substantial gains but have heightened risk and volatility. Investors frequently diversify their portfolios with a mix of these categories, balancing large-caps' stability with smaller coins' growth potential.

Historical fluctuations in market cap provide a window into the dynamic nature of the crypto landscape. Bitcoin's market cap, for instance, has seen exponential growth over the years, reflecting its increasing adoption and acceptance as a store of value. In 2017, Bitcoin's market cap surged to unprecedented levels, fueled by growing mainstream interest and media coverage. Altcoins followed with similar growth, which increased their market cap as investors looked for alternatives to Bitcoin. With its innovative smart contract capabilities, the rise of Ethereum marked a significant milestone as its market cap soared, capturing the imagination of developers and investors alike. These examples illustrate how market cap can shift dramatically due to technological advancements, investor sentiment, and market trends.

Understanding market capitalization and trading volume is crucial for navigating the cryptocurrency market. These metrics offer insights into different cryptocurrencies' size, stability, and liquidity, guiding investment decisions and risk assessments. Whether you're eyeing a large-cap stalwart or a promising small-cap contender, these tools help paint a clearer picture of the market's ever-evolving landscape, ensuring you make informed choices aligned with your financial goals.

How Supply and Demand Affect Crypto Prices

In economics, the law of supply and demand is a fundamental principle that shapes markets, and the cryptocurrency realm is no exception. Imagine a bustling marketplace where the price of goods is determined by how much of a product is available versus how much people want it. In the crypto landscape, this dynamic plays out as investors and enthusiasts drive demand for digital currencies. In contrast, the supply of these currencies can be fixed or vary based on their underlying protocols. When a cryptocurrency has a limited supply, like Bitcoin, the scarcity can drive up prices as more people seek to own a piece of this finite digital asset. Bitcoin's capped supply of 21 million coins makes it akin to digital gold, whose rarity adds intrinsic value. As demand surges, especially during market optimism or economic uncertainty, prices can soar, reflecting the intense competition among buyers.

Fixed versus inflationary supply further illustrates how supply dynamics impact prices. Bitcoin, known for its fixed supply, undergoes halving events approximately every four years. During these events, the reward for mining new blocks is cut in half, reducing the rate at which new Bitcoins enter circulation. This mechanism mimics the scarcity of precious metals and often precedes price rallies, as seen in past halving events. In contrast, cryptocurrencies like Ethereum operate on an inflationary supply model, continually producing new coins. Ethereum's ongoing supply supports its ecosystem's growth, fostering innovation and utility. However, this model can lead to different price dynamics, where balancing supply increases corresponding demand to maintain or elevate prices.

To illustrate the impact of supply and demand on cryptocurrency prices, consider Litecoin. This digital currency shares similarities with Bitcoin but operates on a faster transaction protocol. Like Bitcoin, Litecoin undergoes halving events, historically influencing its price movements. After the 2019 halving, Litecoin experienced a price surge anticipating a reduced new coin supply, followed by a correction as the excitement subsided. This pattern underscores how supply changes, coupled with investor sentiment, can create waves of price volatility. By examining such cases, investors gain insights into how supply metrics can indicate potential price shifts.

Analyzing supply metrics involves more than just understanding the total supply of a cryptocurrency. The circulating supply, representing the number of coins actively traded or held by investors, is crucial in determining market dynamics. A high circulating supply often suggests greater market liquidity, allowing for smoother transactions and potentially moderating price swings. Conversely, a low circulating supply may result in heightened volatility, as fewer coins are available for trading. Investors keen on predicting price movements must evaluate total and circulating supplies, considering factors such as upcoming supply changes, investor behavior, and external market conditions. Understanding these metrics empowers you to navigate the crypto market with insight, recognizing how supply and demand intricacies shape the value of digital currencies.

Cryptocurrencies, as digital assets, offer a unique perspective on the interplay of supply and demand. While traditional markets rely on tangible goods and services, crypto operates within a digital framework where scarcity, utility, and investor psychology converge. By appreciating the nuances of supply metrics and their influence on prices, you gain a clearer view of the forces at play in the crypto space, enabling informed and strategic decision-making. With its dynamic ebb and flow, the digital marketplace continues to evolve, presenting opportunities for those who understand its underlying mechanics.

The Impact of News and Events on Crypto Valuations

So you are on a rollercoaster, where each twist and turn results from news headlines instead of tracks. In the cryptocurrency market, news stories can rapidly send prices soaring or crashing. Regulatory announcements, for instance, often play a pivotal role. When a country announces new regulations, it can instill either confidence or fear among investors. A supportive regulatory environment might lead to a price surge as confidence grows, while strict regulations can spark sell-offs. Consider the impact of high-profile endorsements. When influential figures express support for a particular cryptocurrency, it often increases interest and investment, causing prices to climb. Such endorsements can serve as a catalyst, drawing in new participants who are eager to capitalize on the perceived opportunity.

Social media platforms, especially Twitter, are notorious for influencing crypto volatility. A single tweet from a well-known influencer can ignite significant price changes within minutes. These tweets often spread rapidly, reaching millions of followers worldwide, and can create a domino effect as investors react. Viral news stories, whether factual or speculative, can further magnify this impact, leading to substantial market fluctuations. Information travels like lightning in this digital age, and the cryptocurrency market is susceptible to these rapid shifts. This immediacy makes it crucial for investors to stay informed and discerning, ensuring they separate signals from noise.

Historical events offer a lens through which we can understand the news's profound impact on crypto markets. Take China's regulatory effect on Bitcoin. Over the years, China's stance on cryptocurrency has fluctuated, often causing significant market reactions. Announcements of regulatory crackdowns have historically led to sharp declines in Bitcoin's price, as investors feared the implications of reduced market participation. Similarly, Elon Musk's influence on Dogecoin exemplifies how an individual's actions can sway markets. His tweets and public statements have repeatedly caused Dogecoin's value to spike or plummet, highlighting the power of personality-driven news in the crypto world.

In such a volatile environment, discerning credible news sources is paramount. Relying on reputable crypto news outlets can provide accurate and reliable information, helping investors make informed decisions. These outlets often employ experienced journalists who understand the intricacies of the market and can provide balanced perspectives. Avoiding FUD—fear, uncertainty, and doubt—spreaders is equally essential. These sources often sensationalize or distort information to create panic, leading to rash decisions. Identifying and filtering out such unreliable sources is crucial for anyone in the crypto market. By doing so, investors can navigate the market with a clearer understanding of the factors truly influencing prices.

Common Market Manipulation Tactics to Avoid

In cryptocurrency's vibrant and often unpredictable world, market manipulation can distort the natural ebb and flow of trading. One such tactic is the notorious pump and dump scheme. Here, a group of investors artificially inflates the price of a cryptocurrency by creating a buzz around it. Once the price peaks, these investors sell off their holdings, leaving unsuspecting buyers with significant losses as the price plummets. This tactic relies on generating excitement and urgency, often through misleading information or exaggerated claims, to lure in investors hoping to catch a quick profit. The aftermath is typically a sharp decline in the asset's value, eroding trust and causing financial harm to those seen in the wave.

Another manipulation strategy is spoofing, where traders place large buy or sell orders they have no intention of executing. These orders create a false sense of demand or supply, influencing the price in a desired direction. Once the market reacts, the manipulator cancels these orders, having already capitalized on the price movement. Similarly, wash trading involves an investor buying and selling the same asset multiple times to inflate trading volume artificially. This tactic misleads others into believing there is genuine interest and liquidity in the asset, potentially driving up its price. Both strategies can significantly impact market perceptions, leading to distorted trading volumes and false valuations.

Recognizing the signs of market manipulation is crucial for anyone involved in cryptocurrency trading. Unusual trading volume spikes, for instance, can suggest that a pump-and-dump scheme is underway, especially if there's no news to justify the sudden interest. Similarly, sudden price surges, particularly in lesser-known coins, may indicate manipulation tactics like spoofing. These rapid changes often lack the backing of substantial or credible information and can be temporary. Being vigilant and questioning the motives behind unexpected market movements can help you avoid falling prey to these schemes.

Market manipulation undermines the credibility and stability of crypto markets. It creates a playing field where informed and strategic investors can be blindsided by deceptive practices, leading to a loss of confidence in the market's integrity. When manipulative activities dominate, they hamper genuine price discovery, making the market less predictable and trustworthy. This erosion of investor confidence can deter new entrants and stifle the growth and maturity of the cryptocurrency ecosystem, casting a shadow over the potential benefits these digital assets offer.

Protecting yourself from market manipulation requires a proactive approach. Conduct thorough research before making investment decisions. Dig deep into the fundamentals of a cryptocurrency, examining its use case, team, and community support. Avoid making decisions based solely on hype or fear of missing out. Additionally, consider using limit orders instead of market orders. Limit orders allow you to set the price you are willing to buy or sell, giving you more control over your trades and reducing the impact of sudden market swings. This strategy helps avoid getting caught in artificially inflated price movements and ensures more predictable trading outcomes.

As we use these insights to navigate the cryptocurrency world, remember that knowledge and awareness are your best defenses against market manipulation. By staying informed and exercising caution, you can protect your investments and contribute to a healthier, more transparent market environment. This awareness sets the stage for exploring the intricacies of trading strategies, ensuring you are well-equipped to make informed decisions in the ever-evolving crypto landscape.

Chapter Three

Getting Started with Cryptocurrency

T here's a bustling street market, vibrant with the colors and sounds of vendors selling their goods, each transaction a dance of trust and negotiation. In the digital realm, buying your first Bitcoin echoes this experience, where understanding, security, and careful selection guide you through the process. The thrill of owning a digital currency is akin to holding a rare artifact, a step into a new financial frontier. This chapter will guide you through the essential steps of purchasing Bitcoin and empower you with the knowledge to navigate this new territory with confidence and clarity.

To start, selecting a reputable exchange is crucial. Think of it as choosing a trusted bank or financial advisor. Platforms like Coinbase stand out for beginners due to their user-friendly interfaces and strong security measures, offering a sense of security and peace of mind as you navigate the crypto landscape. Coinbase, renowned for its reliability, provides an intuitive platform where even those new to digital currencies can feel at ease. Consider transaction fees, available cryptocurrencies, and security protocols when choosing a platform. These elements ensure a smooth and secure experience, reducing the risk of unexpected hurdles.

Once you've selected an exchange, the next step is verifying your identity through the KYC process. This step, akin to opening a bank account, ensures compliance with regulations and protects against fraud. You must provide identification documents, such as a passport or driver's license, to verify your identity. While seemingly cumbersome, this process is critical for safeguarding your investment and ensuring your transactions remain secure. Once verified, funding your account with fiat currency becomes the next focus. You can choose from various payment methods, each with pros and cons. Bank transfers, for instance, are secure and often incur lower fees, though they may take longer to process. Credit card purchases offer immediacy but come with higher fees. PayPal provides a middle ground, offering quick transactions with moderate costs. Each method requires careful consideration of your priorities, balancing speed, cost, and security to suit your needs.

Vigilance against scams and fraud is paramount in the cryptocurrency world. Protecting your digital assets is essential, as you would be cautious with your wallet in a crowded market. Phishing websites and fake exchange platforms pose significant risks. Always verify website URLs and avoid clicking on unsolicited links. Research and reviews can help confirm an exchange's legitimacy, ensuring you entrust your funds to a reputable entity. Staying informed and alert minimizes the risk of falling victim to these schemes.

Setting realistic investment goals is vital for a successful foray into cryptocurrency. Consider adopting a long-term holding strategy, where you maintain your investment through market fluctuations, capitalizing on potential future gains. This approach, reminiscent of planting and nurturing a seed over time, can yield significant rewards. Diversification, another prudent strategy, involves spreading your investments across different assets to mitigate risk. Not placing all your eggs in one basket reduces the impact of any single asset's downturn on your overall portfolio. Together, these strategies foster a balanced and strategic approach to investing, allowing you to navigate the crypto market with confidence and foresight.

Checklist to Assist in Secure Bitcoin Buying

- **Research Exchanges**: Ensure they have a strong reputation.

- **Verify Your Identity**: Complete KYC processes diligently.

- **Choose a Payment Method**: Weigh the pros and cons of each option.

- **Stay Alert**: Identify and avoid phishing attempts and fake sites.

- **Set Goals**: Decide on long-term holding and diversification strategies.

This comprehensive approach to buying your first Bitcoin ensures you're well-prepared for the exciting world of cryptocurrency. With careful planning and awareness, you can enjoy the benefits of this digital asset while minimizing risks.

Setting Up a Secure Digital Wallet

In the digital landscape of cryptocurrencies, a secure wallet is your most trusted ally, akin to a vault that holds your financial treasures—choosing the right type of wallet hinges on your unique needs and security preferences. Hot wallets, for instance, cater to those who frequently trade or need instant access to their funds. These wallets, accessible via your smartphone or computer, offer convenience and speed, like having your credit card ready for spontaneous purchases. However, their constant connection to the internet makes them vulnerable to online threats, so use them for smaller amounts you actively trade. On the other hand, cold wallets provide a robust solution for long-term storage. These offline wallets, like hardware wallets, are like a safe deposit box, keeping your assets from prying digital eyes. They are ideal for holding considerable sums without immediate access and provide enhanced security features.

Setting up your digital wallet is a straightforward process. Still, careful attention to detail is required to ensure security from the outset. Start by downloading a reputable wallet application or purchasing a hardware wallet. When you set it up, create a strong password that combines letters, numbers, and symbols to protect your wallet from unauthorized access. Think of it as crafting an unbreakable lock for your safe. Once you set your password, enable additional security features, such as two-factor authentication, which adds an extra layer of protection by requiring a second verification form beyond your password. These measures safeguard your wallet against unwanted intrusions and epitomize the importance of a robust security setup.

Maintaining wallet security is an ongoing commitment. The seed phrase, a string of words generated when you first create your wallet, is crucial. This phrase is the master key to your wallet, allowing you to recover your funds if you lose access. Store it securely and offline, away from digital threats, like keeping the combination safe in a secure location. Another critical aspect of wallet security is guarding against malware. Regularly update your wallet software to patch any vulnerabilities and use antivirus programs to scan your devices. These precautions help ensure that your digital assets remain secure from malicious attacks.

Managing multiple wallets might seem daunting, but it's a valuable strategy for organizing your cryptocurrency holdings. You might choose to have different wallets for distinct purposes, like one for daily transactions and another for long-term investments. Organizing your wallets this way is akin to having separate bank accounts for different financial needs. To efficiently manage these wallets, keep a detailed record of your transactions. Such a record helps you track your spending and investments and simplifies the process come tax season. Many wallets offer built-in tracking features, or you can use dedicated apps to monitor your holdings. Maintaining organized and secure management of your digital wallets ensures that your cryptocurrency investments are accessible and safeguarded, providing peace of mind in the ever-evolving digital financial landscape.

Protecting Your Investments with Two-Factor Authentication

Imagine your digital assets as a treasure stored behind a fortified wall. Traditional security systems, like passwords, serve as the first line of defense. However, a single barrier often isn't enough in a world where cyber threats are rampant. Enter two-factor authentication (2FA), an additional layer of security that makes unauthorized access significantly more challenging. At its core, 2FA requires two different forms of identification before granting access: your password and an additional factor, a one-time code or a biometric scan. This dual-layer system helps to ensure that even if a hacker obtains your password, they still can't access your account without the second factor. It's like having a second lock on your door that requires only a unique key that you possess.

When implementing 2FA, you have choices, such as authentication apps and SMS codes. Authentication apps, like Google Authenticator, generate time-sensitive codes accessible only from your device. They offer a robust security option, as they don't rely on network connections that might be vulnerable to interception. Setting up Google Authenticator is straightforward. Download the app, then link it to your accounts by scanning a QR code provided by the service you're securing. This process generates a unique key on your device, producing a new code every 30 seconds. Backup code management is crucial; these codes act as a lifeline if you lose access to your device, allowing you to regain entry to your account. Store them securely, just as you would a spare house key. SMS codes, while convenient, are less secure, as they are susceptible to SIM-swapping attacks, where a hacker tricks your mobile carrier into transferring your phone number to a new SIM card. Despite this, SMS 2FA still provides a valuable second layer of defense compared to using only a password.

The benefits of 2FA extend beyond simply keeping intruders out. It provides a robust defense against phishing attacks, where malicious actors attempt to trick you into revealing your login details. With 2FA enabled, even if your password is compromised, the attacker can't proceed without the secondary authentication factor. This added layer of safeguarding against unauthorized access offers peace of mind. For investors, this assurance allows you to focus on your financial strategies instead of worrying about potential breaches.

However, 2FA isn't without its challenges. Losing access to your 2FA device, such as your phone, can be a significant inconvenience. Preparing for such scenarios is essential to understanding the recovery process in advance. Most platforms offer backup codes generated when you set up 2FA. These codes should be printed or written down and kept in a safe place, separate from your digital devices. Additionally, some services allow you to register multiple devices for 2FA, providing an alternative if your primary device is lost or stolen. Understanding these options can help you quickly regain access and minimize disruption

While 2FA adds complexity to the login process, the security benefits far outweigh the minor inconvenience. Embracing this technology means proactively protecting your digital investments, ensuring that your accounts remain secure against the growing threat of cybercrime. By anticipating challenges and learning how to navigate them, you're not just safeguarding your assets—you're also enhancing your confidence and control in the cryptocurrency space.

Choosing the Right Exchange for You

You're setting out to choose a new bank. You'd want one that keeps your money safe and offers services that match your financial needs. The same applies when selecting a cryptocurrency exchange. Security measures should be top of mind. A reputable exchange, like Coinbase or Gemini, uses robust security protocols to protect your investments. Look for features like two-factor authentication, cold storage of funds, and insurance policies against breaches. An exchange's reputation is equally important. Research user reviews, check for any previous security incidents, and consider the platform's track record. For peace of mind, choose an exchange consistently demonstrating transparency and reliability.

Another crucial factor is the range of supported cryptocurrencies and trading pairs. To explore beyond Bitcoin, consider an exchange offering diverse digital assets. Platforms like Kraken or Crypto.com provide a wide array of cryptocurrencies, allowing you to diversify your portfolio. Evaluate the trading pairs available, as some exchanges may not offer direct conversions between lesser-known coins. This variety broadens your investment opportunities and provides flexibility in managing your assets. By aligning your preferences with the exchange's offerings, you can ensure that your trading experience meets your expectations.

When comparing centralized and decentralized exchanges, it's essential to understand their differences. Centralized exchanges, like Binance, operate with a middleman facilitating trades and often provide greater liquidity. This liquidity ensures you can buy or sell assets quickly without significantly affecting the market price. However, trust in the platform is required to safeguard your funds. Decentralized exchanges, such as Uniswap, eliminate intermediaries, enabling direct peer-to-peer transactions. They offer increased privacy and control over your assets. Yet, decentralized platforms may suffer from lower liquidity and potentially higher volatility. Your choice depends on your priorities—whether you value liquidity and ease of use or prefer control and privacy.

User experience plays a pivotal role in your interaction with an exchange. A platform with an intuitive interface can simplify the trading process. Look for features like clear navigation menus, real-time market data, and customizable dashboards. These elements enhance your ability to make informed decisions swiftly. Reliable customer support is another aspect to consider. An exchange with responsive support can assist you in resolving issues quickly, ensuring uninterrupted trading. Additionally, exchanges offering educational resources, such as tutorials and webinars, can be invaluable for beginners. These resources enhance your market understanding, enabling more strategic investment choices.

Evaluating exchange fees and limits is key to managing your costs effectively. Exchanges typically charge transaction fees that vary based on the trading volume or type of transaction. For instance, platforms like Kraken offer lower fees for high-volume traders, making it advantageous for those engaging in frequent trades. Understanding these fee structures helps you anticipate costs and factor them into your investment strategy. Withdrawal limits are another consideration. Some exchanges impose minimum deposit requirements or withdrawal thresholds, impacting your ability to access funds. By thoroughly reviewing these details, you can choose an exchange that aligns with your financial goals and minimizes unnecessary expenses.

Avoiding Common Mistakes When Transferring Crypto

Transferring cryptocurrency is like sending a valuable package through the mail. You want to ensure it reaches its destination safely and securely without any hiccups along the way. The first and most crucial step is double-checking wallet addresses before initiating a transaction. Think of the address as the recipient's postal address; a single mistake could mean your package goes to the wrong place or gets lost entirely. Always copy and paste the wallet address and verify it by checking the first and last few characters. This simple step can prevent costly errors and ensure your crypto ends where you intend.

Before committing to a large transfer, consider sending a test transaction. This involves sending a small amount of cryptocurrency to the intended address to confirm everything is accurate. It's like sending a postcard to verify an address before mailing a critical letter. Once the test transaction is successful, you can proceed with the complete transfer, confident that it will arrive as expected. This precaution may seem tedious, but it offers significant peace of mind, knowing that your assets are secure.

Common mistakes during transfers often stem from simple oversights. Copy-paste errors, where an extra space or character appears, can lead to failed transactions. To avoid this, always double-check the pasted address before confirming the transfer. Another common issue is misunderstanding transaction fees. Each transfer incurs a fee, depending on the network's congestion and the amount sent. Be sure to account for these fees, as failing can result in insufficient funds and a failed transaction. Understanding these fees helps you plan your transfers better and avoid unexpected costs.

The concept of network confirmations is integral to cryptocurrency transfers. When you send crypto, the transaction needs to be confirmed by the network, similar to how a bank processes a check before the funds are available. The number of confirmations required depends on the cryptocurrency and the exchange or wallet policies. For example, Bitcoin transactions typically need six confirmations to be considered secure. Each confirmation involves the transaction being recorded in a new block on the blockchain, adding layers of security. Ensuring receipt of the required number of confirmations before considering the complete transfer protects you from double-spending and potential fraud.

Even with careful planning, transfer issues can occur. A common problem is a stuck transaction, where the transfer remains unconfirmed for an extended period. Setting the transaction fee too low can deprioritize its status on the network. To resolve this, you might try "fee bumping," which involves increasing the transaction fee to expedite processing. Alternatively, some wallets offer a "Replace by Fee" option, allowing you to resend the transaction at a higher cost. Familiarizing yourself with these solutions ensures you can handle transfer issues efficiently, minimizing disruption to your crypto activities.

Backing Up Your Wallet to Ensure Peace of Mind

In cryptocurrency, backing up your wallet is like creating a safety net, ensuring that your digital assets remain secure even in unforeseen circumstances. Consider the seed phrase—often a string of 12 to 24 words—generated when you set up your wallet. This phrase is the master key, granting access to your funds if the wallet is lost or compromised. It is imperative to store your seed phrase securely. Please write it down on paper and store it in a waterproof and fireproof safe, or use a metal backup plate designed to withstand physical damage. Avoid digital storage options like cloud services, which are susceptible to hacking. This precaution ensures that even if your device fails, your assets remain accessible.

Creating secure backups involves more than just safeguarding your seed phrase. It's about storing multiple copies in different locations to protect against loss or damage. Consider keeping one copy in a safe at home and another in a bank deposit box. Some people even split the phrase into parts, storing each separately to enhance security. Additionally, encrypt digital backups if you store them on secure USB drives. Encryption adds a layer of protection, making the data unreadable without the correct passphrase. This multi-layered backup approach minimizes the risk of losing access to your assets due to unforeseen events like theft or natural disasters.

Hardware wallets are integral in securing your digital assets, serving as a robust backup solution. These devices keep your private keys offline, shielding you against online threats like hacking and malware. Maintaining your assets in cold storage significantly reduces the risk of unauthorized access. Hardware wallets are advantageous for long-term holders, as they balance security and convenience. With a simple connection to your computer via USB, you can access your funds when needed, while keeping them protected during idle periods. Hardware wallets are an excellent choice for safely storing a substantial amount of cryptocurrency over time.

Regularly updating your backups is as important as creating them. Wallets and cryptocurrencies evolve, and so can your digital assets' requirements. Periodically reviewing your backup solutions ensures they remain effective and aligned with any changes in your holdings. Set reminders to check your backups every few months, verifying that all copies are intact and stored securely. If you acquire new cryptocurrencies or update your wallet, create new backups to reflect these changes. This practice protects your current assets. It also keeps you prepared for future developments in the crypto space. By keeping your backups current, you maintain peace of mind, knowing your digital wealth is consistently protected.

As we conclude this chapter, remember that securing and managing your cryptocurrency holdings is a dynamic process requiring diligence and foresight. Proper backups, secure storage solutions, and regular updates form the foundation of a sound strategy for safeguarding your investments. With these tools and practices, you can confidently navigate the evolving landscape of digital finance, prepared for current and future challenges. The next chapter will delve into the intricacies of developing a trading strategy, equipping you with the knowledge to grow your investments wisely and strategically.

Chapter Four

Developing a Trading Strategy

E nvision an ancient ship navigating the vast, unpredictable ocean, the captain steering with a steady hand, charting a course through the tempestuous waters. In the cryptocurrency world, you are that captain, guiding your investments through the financial seas with a keen eye on the horizon. As you delve into the complexities of trading strategies, you'll find that a solid anchor can provide stability amidst the volatility. This chapter begins by exploring the HODL philosophy. This steadfast approach has become a cornerstone for many in the crypto community.

The term "HODL" emerged from a typo in a 2013 forum post during a Bitcoin market dip, where a user named GameKyuubi defiantly declared, "I AM HODLING." This accidental misspelling became a battle cry for crypto investors, symbolizing the practice of holding on to assets through the market's ups and downs. "HODLING" is akin to the traditional buy-and-hold strategy familiar in stock markets, where investors resist the urge to sell during downturns, instead focusing on long-term growth potential. This philosophy encourages you to view your investments as enduring commitments, weathering the market's inevitable fluctuations with patience and resolve. By adopting this mindset, you align yourself with the belief that the market will trend upward over time, rewarding those who maintain their composure and confidence.

One of the most compelling benefits of a long-term approach like HODL is the potential for substantial returns. Despite their volatility, cryptocurrencies have shown remarkable growth over the years. By holding on to your assets, you position yourself to reap the rewards of this appreciation without the stress of trying to time the market perfectly. This potential for significant returns should fill you with optimism and hope for your investment journey. Additionally, long-term holding reduces transaction costs. Every trade incurs fees, and by minimizing your trades, you save on these costs, allowing more of your capital to remain invested. This approach also frees you from the constant monitoring and decision-making that short-term trading demands, offering a more hands-off investment strategy that builds discipline and resilience.

When considering which cryptocurrencies to use for HODL, focus on established coins like Bitcoin and Ethereum. These digital assets have demonstrated resilience and growth potential, becoming mainstays in the crypto landscape. With its capped supply and widespread recognition, Bitcoin is a digital store of value akin to gold. Ethereum, known for its innovative contract capabilities and robust ecosystem, offers growth opportunities through innovation and application development. These attributes make them suitable candidates for long-term holding, providing a foundation of stability and potential that aligns with the HODL philosophy.

Staying committed to your HODL plan requires setting clear long-term goals. Define what you hope to achieve with your investments, whether funding a future purchase, preparing for retirement, or building generational wealth. These goals serve as guiding stars, helping you navigate the market's turbulence with purpose and clarity. Setting clear long-term goals should make you feel focused and determined in your investment strategy. Additionally, learn to ignore short-term market noise. Daily price fluctuations can be distracting and may tempt you to react impulsively. Instead, focus on the broader trends and the reasons you invested in the first place. By keeping your eyes on the long-term horizon, you cultivate patience and avoid emotional trading pitfalls.

Take a Moment

- Pause and jot down your long-term financial goals and how they align with your current crypto holdings.

- Reflect on why you chose these specific assets and what you hope to achieve by holding them.

- Consider setting reminders to revisit these thoughts periodically, reinforcing your commitment to the HODL strategy.

As you continue to develop your trading strategy, remember that the HODL philosophy is about more than just holding assets—it's about building a mindset that embraces the long-term journey, trusting in the potential of cryptocurrency to transform your financial future. And trust in cryptocurrency's potential.

Basic Trading Strategy: Buy Low, Sell High

In cryptocurrency trading, buying low and selling high is one of the most fundamental concepts. This strategy is straightforward: purchase low-price assets and sell them when they rise, capturing the difference as profit. It is essential to precisely identify market entry and exit points, much like timing the perfect moment to catch a wave. Engaging in this strategy requires a keen understanding of market trends, insights into price movements, and the ability to make decisions based on data rather than emotion. The allure lies in its simplicity, yet the execution demands discipline and foresight.

Timing the market, however, presents its own set of challenges. Cryptocurrency volatility can make predicting the best times to buy and sell a daunting task. Psychological barriers often come into play, where fear and greed can cloud judgment, leading to hasty decisions. These emotions can cause you to buy at the peak, fearing missing out on gains or selling in a panic during downturns. However, patience becomes a crucial ally in this scenario. It allows you to wait for the right conditions rather than reacting impulsively. Embracing patience should reassure you and instill confidence in your ability to make strategic and calculated trading decisions, mitigating the emotional rollercoaster that market fluctuations can cause.

The annals of cryptocurrency history include numerous tales of successful buy-low and sell-high trades. Bitcoin's meteoric rise in 2017 serves as a textbook example. Early adopters who purchased Bitcoin when it hovered around a few hundred dollars reaped substantial profits as it surged to nearly $20,000 by the end of the year. Similarly, Ethereum's early supporters found themselves in an enviable position when the platform gained traction and its value skyrocketed. These stories highlight the potential rewards of timing the market correctly, turning modest investments into significant financial gains. Other examples include the rise of Ripple's XRP in 2017, which saw its value increase by over 35,000% in a single year, and the surge of Binance Coin (BNB) in 2019, which saw its value increase by over 500% in just a few months. These examples underscore the importance of foresight and a willingness to endure periods of uncertainty.

Implementing the buy low, sell high strategy effectively involves several practical steps. First, consider setting target prices for your trades. Determine the price you are comfortable buying and the level at which you plan to sell. Setting these targets ahead of time can help you avoid impulsive decisions driven by market hype or fear. Another powerful tool in this strategy is the use of limit orders. A limit order allows you to set a specific price for buying or selling, ensuring that the trade only executes according to your conditions. For instance, if you want to buy a cryptocurrency when it reaches a specific low price, you can set a buy limit order at that price. Similarly, you can set a sell limit order if you intend to sell when the price reaches a specific high. This approach provides more control over your transactions, reducing the risk of entering or exiting the market at suboptimal times. Limit orders can benefit volatile markets, where prices can swing rapidly. Setting them establishes a buffer against emotional trading, sticking to your predefined strategy.

A Reflection Exercise

- Reflect on a past investment decision and consider how patience or impulsivity played a role.

- What factors influenced your timing, and what would you do differently in hindsight?

- Writing this down can help reinforce the importance of discipline and planning in your future trading endeavors.

While the buy low, sell high strategy offers profit opportunities, it requires a balance of patience, discipline, and informed decision-making. Embracing these principles can help you navigate the complexities of crypto trading, potentially leading to successful outcomes.

Diversifying Your Crypto Portfolio

Picture yourself walking through a vibrant vegetable market. Each stall offers a different array of produce, and as you fill your basket, you're not just choosing the juiciest apples or the freshest greens. You're spreading your selections to ensure a balanced and nutritious meal. This analogy holds for cryptocurrency investments, where diversification becomes a crucial strategy to manage risk and enhance potential returns. By not putting all your eggs in one basket, you reduce exposure to the volatility of any single asset. In the crypto market, which is notorious for its price swings, this strategy helps stabilize your portfolio, minimizing the impact when one particular asset dives.

Creating a well-rounded crypto portfolio involves strategically selecting various digital assets. Start by including a mix of large-cap cryptocurrencies like Bitcoin and Ethereum. These are like blue-chip stocks, offering stability and a solid foundation due to their established market presence. Adding altcoins can inject growth potential into your portfolio; they are often more volatile but yield higher returns. Striking a balance between risk and reward is key.

Stablecoins, such as Tether or USD Coin, are another essential component in a diversified portfolio. These digital currencies are pegged to traditional fiat currencies, offering a stable value in a sea of crypto volatility. They act as a financial anchor, providing liquidity and hedging against sudden market downturns. For instance, during a market dip, holding stablecoins can prevent the erosion of your portfolio's value, enabling you to buy other assets at lower prices when the market begins to recover. Including stablecoins in your portfolio provides a buffer, ensuring you maintain stability amidst the unpredictable waves of the crypto market.

To illustrate the principles of diversification, let's consider some sample portfolio allocations. A conservative approach might involve dedicating 60% of your investments to Bitcoin, leveraging its reputation and relative stability. With its robust ecosystem and potential for growth, Ethereum could occupy 25% of your portfolio. The remaining 15% could be spread across promising altcoins, offering exposure to various sectors within the crypto space, such as decentralized finance (DeFi) or non-fungible tokens (NFTs). This allocation ensures that while the core of your portfolio remains secure, you still have the opportunity to capitalize on emerging trends and technologies.

In the dynamic realm of cryptocurrency, diversification is not merely a strategy; it's a necessity. By thoughtfully selecting a mixture of assets, you mitigate risk and position yourself to capture gains in different market conditions. This balanced approach allows you to navigate the crypto market with stability, ensuring that your financial aspirations can withstand the test of time.

Understanding Stop-Loss and Take-Profit Orders

When trading cryptocurrencies, managing risk is crucial. Stop-loss and take-profit orders are vital tools in this process, acting like safety nets that protect your investments. A stop-loss order automatically sells a portion of your holdings if the price falls to a predetermined level. This mechanism helps prevent significant losses by exiting a position before it plummets further. Think of it as an emergency brake on a rollercoaster, halting the ride before it spirals out of control. Conversely, a take-profit order locks in gains by selling when the price reaches a high point, ensuring you secure the profits before market conditions can reverse. Both orders allow you to set trade boundaries, providing a structured approach to managing your assets.

Determining the proper levels for these orders requires a blend of technical analysis and market understanding. Technical analysis involves studying past price movements and chart patterns to forecast future trends. Examining support and resistance levels allows you to identify logical points to set your stop-loss and take-profit limits. For example, setting a stop-loss just below a strong support level can minimize the risk of being stopped in a temporary dip. Similarly, a take-profit order near a resistance level may capture gains before encountering selling pressure. However, market conditions are ever-changing, and adapting your order levels is crucial. You might opt for wider stop-loss margins during volatile periods to accommodate more significant price swings. Conversely, tighter limits can be appropriate in stable markets with minimal fluctuations.

Utilizing stop-loss and take-profit orders can significantly enhance your trading discipline. These automated tools reduce the emotional component of trading, which often leads to impulsive decisions. Without constantly monitoring prices, you can alleviate stress and focus on broader market strategies. Knowing your investments are protected gives you peace of mind, allowing you to approach trading with a clear head, free from the anxiety of potential losses or missed opportunities. This systematic approach establishes a structured trading environment using knowledge-based decisions based on predefined criteria rather than transient emotions.

Consider the example of a trader during a market downturn. By employing stop-loss orders, the trader can limit losses as prices fall, preserving capital for future opportunities. This approach prevents panic selling and maintains a strategic stance, ready to re-enter the market when conditions improve. On the flip side, after a significant price spike, a take-profit order can secure gains before the market retracts. This proactive strategy captures value at its peak, realizing profits without the temptation to hold for potentially higher but uncertain returns.

Stop-loss and take-profit orders are essential components of a well-rounded trading strategy. They provide a framework for making informed decisions and balancing risk and reward in dynamic markets. By setting these parameters, you create a safety net for your investments, allowing you to navigate the unpredictable world of cryptocurrency trading confidently.

Protecting Your Investments with Risk Management

Risk management is an unwavering pillar of successful trading in the unpredictable world of cryptocurrency. Picture a tightrope walker balancing precariously above the ground. Without a safety net, one misstep could lead to disaster. Similarly, effective risk management acts as that safety net in trading, preserving your capital and ensuring consistent growth over time. It's not merely about avoiding losses—it's about setting the stage for future success by protecting your assets against the market's capricious turns. By focusing on risk management, you safeguard your portfolio's longevity, allowing it to weather storms and thrive in calmer waters.

One of the primary strategies in managing risk involves position sizing, which determines how much of your capital to allocate to a particular trade. Imagine each trade as a bet—bet too much, and a loss could wipe you out; bet too little, and you might not gain enough to justify the risk. Position sizing helps strike a balance, ensuring that no single trade can significantly damage your portfolio. It's a calculated approach to investment, where you decide the proportion of your total capital to risk on any given trade based on your confidence in the trade and the potential impact of a loss. Maintaining disciplined position sizes mitigates the risk of substantial losses, keeping your portfolio diversified and resilient.

Diversification across asset classes is another cornerstone of risk management. Just as a gardener plants various crops to ensure a harvest regardless of weather conditions, diversifying your investments spreads risk and increases opportunities for returns. Likewise, investing in multiple cryptocurrencies and considering other asset classes like stocks, bonds, or real estate. By allocating your investments across various sectors, you reduce the impact of a downturn in any single area. Diversification ensures that while one market may falter, others may flourish, providing a buffer against volatility and enhancing overall portfolio stability.

The concept of the risk-reward ratio is a powerful tool for evaluating potential trades. It compares your risk with the potential reward you anticipate earning. Calculating this ratio involves estimating the potential profit of a trade and comparing it to the potential loss. For instance, a 3:1 risk-reward ratio indicates that you aim to gain three dollars for every dollar you risk. Setting favorable risk-reward targets helps ensure that your potential gains outweigh potential losses, guiding you to make informed, strategic decisions. This disciplined approach encourages you to pursue only those trades where the reward justifies the risk, fostering a mindset of prudence and calculated boldness.

Consider the effectiveness of risk management through real-world scenarios. During sharp market downturns, traders implementing robust risk management strategies avoided catastrophic losses. By setting stop-loss orders and adhering to position sizing rules, they preserved their capital, allowing them to re-enter the market when conditions improved. This foresight enabled them to maintain a foothold in the market, ready to capitalize on future opportunities. In contrast, those without such strategies often found themselves sidelined, with depleted resources and diminished prospects. Effective risk management thus acts as a shield, protecting your investments and positioning you for sustained success in the dynamic world of cryptocurrency.

Avoiding the FOMO Trap of Emotional Trading

In the fast-paced world of cryptocurrency, the fear of missing out, commonly known as FOMO, can be a powerful driver of behavior. FOMO is that nagging sensation when you see a digital asset skyrocketing in value and you're not a part of it. This emotional response can lead to impulsive decisions, pushing you to buy at inflated prices or sell in a panic. The mere sight of a sudden surge on a trading chart can make it feel like everyone else is profiting while you stand by helplessly. This urgency often stems from media-driven narratives that paint a picture of unstoppable gains, making it seem like a once-in-a-lifetime opportunity is slipping through your fingers.

Emotional triggers in trading are plentiful and can be as sudden as a lightning bolt. A sharp price spike might catch your attention, filling your mind with visions of quick profits. Yet, these spikes are often volatile, riding on waves of speculation rather than solid fundamentals. Media outlets frequently amplify this hype, with headlines proclaiming massive gains or potential crashes. With their rapid-fire updates, social media platforms fuel the fire, creating a cacophony of voices that can overwhelm your better judgment. In such an environment, it's easy to become swept up in the frenzy, making decisions based on fear and excitement rather than careful analysis.

Developing a trading plan is crucial to navigate the noise and keep FOMO at bay. A well-structured plan acts as a compass, guiding decisions with predetermined criteria rather than spur-of-the-moment reactions. It includes setting straightforward entry and exit points based on your research and risk tolerance, not market chatter. Practicing mindfulness can also serve as a powerful tool. By cultivating self-awareness, you can recognize when emotions cloud your judgment and take a step back to reassess. Take a moment to breathe, reflect on your goals, or remind yourself of the long-term nature of your investments. These practices help anchor you amidst the market's ups and downs, fostering rational decision-making.

Consider the story of a trader who bought Bitcoin during its peak in late 2017. Driven by FOMO, they invested as prices soared, fueled by the belief that the upward trend would continue indefinitely. However, when the market corrected, they faced substantial losses, having bought at an unsustainable high. Similarly, panic selling during market corrections is a common pitfall. Imagine a trader who sells their holdings at the first sign of a downturn, only to watch the market recover shortly after. These cautionary tales illustrate the detrimental impact of FOMO, where quick decisions lead to regret and financial setbacks.

In crypto trading, emotions can be both an ally and an adversary. Recognizing the influence of FOMO and implementing strategies to manage it can prevent costly mistakes. Focusing on a disciplined approach grounded in a clear plan and self-awareness allows you to navigate the market with greater confidence and stability.

This chapter has explored strategies to enhance your trading mindset, setting the stage for more informed and deliberate investment decisions. As you prepare to delve into the next chapter, consider how these strategies can be applied to further refine your approach to cryptocurrency.

Chapter Five

Security and Fraud Prevention

There's a vibrant marketplace, alive with the shouts of vendors and the eager sifting of customers. In this bustling scene, a cunning pickpocket preys on the unsuspecting. The digital bazaar of the cryptocurrency world is no different, with scams operating with similar guile, targeting both seasoned investors and newcomers. As you navigate this digital landscape, the importance of safeguarding your assets from scams cannot be overstated. Just as you would protect your wallet in a crowded street, it's crucial to recognize and steer clear of the common crypto scams that lurk in the shadows.

Scammers frequently disguise Ponzi schemes as legitimate investment platforms, promising high returns with little risk. These schemes rely on new investors' funds to pay existing members, creating an illusion of profitability until the influx of new money dries up. Such platforms often boast guaranteed returns, an enticing prospect that should immediately raise suspicion. Genuine investments carry inherent risks, and any promise to the contrary warrants cautious scrutiny. The lack of transparency further marks these schemes. They often operate behind a veil of secrecy, providing little verifiable information about their operations or the people behind them. This is where your healthy skepticism can be your best defense.

Fake Initial Coin Offerings (ICOs) present another common trap, exploiting the excitement surrounding new cryptocurrency projects. These scams mimic legitimate fundraising efforts, luring investors with the promise of getting in on the ground floor of the next big thing. However, they often vanish once funds are collected, leaving investors with worthless tokens. A hallmark of these scams is their reliance on slick marketing and vague, jargon-filled pitches that lack substance. Authentic ICOs involve detailed whitepapers and clear business plans, providing insight into the project's viability and potential returns.

The collapse of Bitconnect serves as a stark reminder of the perils associated with crypto scams. Marketed as a high-yield investment program, Bitconnect promised staggering returns through its lending program. However, it operated as a classic Ponzi scheme, ultimately collapsing and causing significant financial losses for thousands of investors. Similarly, the OneCoin pyramid scheme enticed investors worldwide with promises of immense wealth, only to be exposed as one of the largest crypto frauds in history. These examples underscore the importance of vigilance and skepticism in the face of too-good-to-be-true offers.

To shield yourself from scams, conducting comprehensive background checks is essential. Investigate the platform's history, scrutinize the team behind it, and verify their credentials. Reputable projects often have a transparent track record and a team with verifiable experience in the industry. Equally important is to be wary of unsolicited offers. Scammers often resort to aggressive marketing tactics, pressuring potential victims to act quickly. Exercise caution, take your time to research, and seek advice from trusted sources before making investment decisions. By remaining vigilant and well-informed, you can protect yourself from falling victim to fraudulent schemes.

A Scam Spotting Exercise

To sharpen your abilities in identifying potential scams within the cryptocurrency space, it's prudent to develop a comprehensive checklist of warning signs. This checklist should serve as your go-to guide when assessing new investment opportunities. Key elements to include in your scam detection toolkit are:

- **Promises of Guaranteed Returns**: Be wary of any investment that offers guaranteed profits. The volatile nature of cryptocurrencies means returns cannot and should not be guaranteed.

- **Lack of Verifiable Information**: Legitimate projects have transparent operations and provide ample information about their team, technology, and progress. A scarcity of accessible, verifiable details should raise concerns.

- **Pressure to Invest Quickly**: Scammers often create a sense of urgency, suggesting that missing out would result in a lost opportunity. Real opportunities are based on thorough research, not rushed decisions.

- **Unrealistic Profit Projections**: Be cautious of projects that claim you can "double your investment overnight." Cryptocurrency markets can offer significant returns, but they come with equally significant risks.

- **Anonymous Teams**: Knowing who is behind a project can add a layer of trust. Projects that hide their team's identity could be a red flag.

- **Complicated or Non-Existent Whitepapers**: A project's whitepaper should clearly explain its purpose, technology, and roadmap. If a whitepaper is overly complex, vague, or missing altogether, it might be a scheme to defraud investors.

Incorporating these elements into your checklist will enhance your vigilance and help safeguard your investments against the myriads of scams prevalent in the cryptocurrency market. Always approach new investment opportunities with a critical eye, leveraging your checklist to ensure you make informed, cautious decisions in your cryptocurrency journey.

Keeping Your Assets Safe: Best Security Practices

Securing your digital assets begins with a fundamental approach—strong, unique passwords. Imagine your password as the key to a vault. It needs to be intricate enough to prevent unauthorized access. Avoid using easily guessed words or personal information. Instead, craft a complex combination of letters, numbers, and symbols. This strategy is a formidable barrier against those attempting to breach your accounts. Changing passwords regularly adds another layer of security, ensuring that it won't lead to significant losses even if one is compromised. Consider using a password manager to keep track of these complex keys, reducing the risk of forgetting them while maintaining the highest security standards.

Implementing multifactor authentication (MFA) acts the same as adding a deadbolt to the vault's door. It requires a password and an additional verification form, like a code sent to your phone or a biometric scan. This second step significantly reduces the chances of unauthorized access, as it requires something only you possess. Think of it as a fail-safe, ensuring that even if a hacker obtains your password, they still can't breach your defenses without the second factor. Setting up MFA is straightforward and well worth the effort for the peace of mind it provides.

Antivirus software is crucial in protecting your devices from malware and cyber threats. These programs act as vigilant guards, constantly scanning for and neutralizing threats before they can cause harm. Regular updates are vital, as they ensure your software can combat the latest threats. Think of these updates as vaccinations, keeping your system healthy and resilient. Scheduled scans should be a routine part of your digital hygiene, much like regular check-ups with a doctor. Keeping your antivirus software up-to-date creates a robust line of defense that protects your assets from malicious attacks.

Another crucial aspect of digital security is the use of secure networks. While public Wi-Fi is convenient, it can be a breeding ground for cybercriminals looking to intercept data. It's like leaving your front door open on a busy street. For sensitive transactions, always opt for secure, private internet connections. If you must use public Wi-Fi, consider setting up a Virtual Private Network (VPN). A VPN encrypts your data, making it nearly impossible for others to eavesdrop on your activities. A VPN is a secure tunnel through which your data travels, safe from prying eyes. This approach ensures that your online activities remain private and your assets secure, even in less controlled environments.

Securing your mobile devices is equally important, as they often serve as the gateways to your cryptocurrency holdings. Enable device encryption to protect the data stored on your phone or tablet. Encryption scrambles your data, rendering it unreadable without the decryption key. It's like locking your valuables in a safe, only accessible with the correct combination. Additionally, install security apps that offer features like remote wiping, which allows you to erase your data if your device is lost or stolen. These apps often come with additional tools, such as malware protection and safe browsing features, further bolstering your device's defenses.

These security measures establish a strong defense system, safeguarding your digital assets from many threats. Adopting this vigilant stance not only ensures the safety and accessibility of your cryptocurrency investments but also fosters a secure environment for your financial growth. In the ever-evolving landscape of the digital marketplace, being proactive and continuously informed is paramount. By staying alert and knowledgeable about the latest security practices, you significantly enhance the protection of your investments. Remember, the safety of your digital assets lies in your hands; maintaining constant vigilance is key to ensuring their security and, by extension, the health of your financial future.

How to Verify the Legitimacy of a Crypto Project

Imagine you're considering a new investment in the cryptocurrency world. The excitement of a promising project can be overwhelming, but it's crucial to proceed with caution. Conducting due diligence is your first line of defense. Examine the project's whitepaper, the blueprint for its vision and technology. A well-crafted whitepaper should articulate the project's goals, the problem it aims to solve, and the technical framework it will employ. Look for clarity and detail—vague promises or overly technical jargon without substance are red flags. A sound whitepaper should give you a clear understanding of the project's potential and how it plans to achieve its objectives.

Next, delve into the development team's background. The team behind a project is as important as the technology itself. Research the team's previous work, industry experience, and notable achievements. LinkedIn can be a helpful tool for verifying professional credentials. A team with a proven track record in technology and business development adds credibility to the project.

On the other hand, if the team is anonymous or lacks verifiable experience, proceed with caution. Transparency about the team's identity and experience is often a good indicator of the project's legitimacy. Trustworthy projects will proudly present their team members and advisors, demonstrating their commitment to accountability and success.

Community feedback offers invaluable insights into a project's credibility. Platforms like Reddit and Bitcointalk are bustling forums where crypto enthusiasts and experts discuss the merits and pitfalls of various projects. Engaging in these discussions can reveal community sentiment and uncover potential issues that may not be immediately apparent. Additionally, Trustpilot reviews can provide an overview of user experiences and satisfaction. While positive reviews can be reassuring, please pay close attention to any recurring negative feedback, as it might highlight persistent problems or shortcomings. A project with strong, positive community engagement usually indicates a healthy and transparent relationship with its supporters.

Regulatory compliance is another critical aspect to consider when verifying a crypto project. Ensure the project adheres to relevant legal standards and possesses necessary licenses or registrations. Checking helps mitigate regulatory intervention risk, which can disrupt or even halt a project's progress. Legitimate projects will often display their compliance status on their website, signaling their commitment to operating within legal boundaries. Checking for compliance can protect you from potential legal repercussions and ensure the project's long-term viability. In an industry where regulations continually evolve, a project's willingness to comply reflects its adaptability and dedication to sustainable growth.

Examples of successful crypto initiatives can provide benchmarks for assessing new projects. Ethereum, for instance, has become a cornerstone of the crypto ecosystem thanks to its robust development and widespread adoption. Its open-source platform enables developers to create decentralized applications, showcasing the power of a clear vision and technical prowess. Cardano, another prominent project, distinguishes itself with a strong academic foundation. It emphasizes peer-reviewed research and a methodical approach to development, instilling confidence in its innovative capabilities. These projects exemplify how transparency, technical soundness, and community support contribute to legitimacy and success in the crypto sphere. By learning from these examples, you can better assess the potential of new projects you encounter in your investment journey.

Understanding Phishing Attacks and How to Avoid Them

Picture this: you're checking your email, and a message from what seems to be your cryptocurrency exchange urges immediate action to avoid account suspension. The email looks legitimate, complete with logos and official-sounding language. But this is a phishing attempt—a deceptive tactic to steal sensitive information. In the realm of cryptocurrency, phishing poses a significant threat. Cybercriminals craft emails or SMS messages that mimic trusted entities, aiming to trick you into revealing passwords, private keys, or other personal information. These attacks can lead to unauthorized access to your crypto assets, with potentially devastating consequences.

Phishers employ various tactics to deceive and manipulate. One standard method involves spoofed websites, where criminals create fake sites that closely resemble legitimate ones. When you unwittingly enter your credentials, they capture your information for malicious use. Another tactic is impersonating service providers through emails or phone calls, claiming issues with your account, or offering technical support. These imposters often use urgent language to pressure you into sharing information. The sophistication of these schemes can easily mislead even the cautious, underscoring the importance of vigilance.

To protect yourself against phishing, verify URLs before clicking any links. Hover over the link to view the web address and ensure it matches a legitimate site. Phishers often use slight variations in domain names to trick users. Avoid clicking links or downloading attachments from unknown sources, as they might contain malware to harvest your data. Additionally, be wary of sharing sensitive information over the phone or through email. Reputable companies rarely request such details this way. Maintaining a healthy skepticism and verifying requests through official channels builds a strong line of defense against phishing attempts.

Consider these real-world examples: In 2018, a phishing attack targeted Binance users through fake websites, successfully capturing login credentials and API keys. The attackers then used this information to manipulate the market, causing many losses. Similarly, phishing emails masquerading as Ledger, a popular hardware wallet, deceived users into providing their recovery phrases. With these details, scammers gained full access to victims' wallets, leading to significant financial theft. These incidents highlight the high stakes involved and the need for constant vigilance.

Phishing remains a prevalent threat in cryptocurrency. However, understanding its tactics and being cautious can significantly reduce your risk. Stay informed about the latest phishing trends and educate yourself on the signs of potential attacks. Regularly update your security practices and remain skeptical of unexpected communications, especially those that urge immediate action. Doing so can protect your digital assets and navigate the crypto space with greater confidence and security.

Cold Storage Solutions: Taking Your Security to the Next Level

Imagine a deep underground vault where treasures are stored far from prying eyes and digital threats. Such is the essence of cold storage in the cryptocurrency world. Cold storage refers to keeping private keys, which are the keys to accessing your digital assets, entirely offline. This method drastically reduces the risks associated with online hacks, as it removes your assets from the reach of malicious actors lurking in cyberspace. Cold storage serves as a fortress, protecting your digital wealth by ensuring your private keys are inaccessible to anyone without physical access to your storage medium.

There are several methods to implement cold storage, each with its advantages. Hardware wallets like Trezor and Ledger are among the most popular choices. These devices are similar to USB drives, securely storing your private keys offline. Manufacturers design them to be user-friendly, allowing you to easily access your cryptocurrencies while keeping them safe from online threats. Another option is the paper wallet, which prints your private and public keys on paper. While more vulnerable to physical damage, this method offers a cost-effective way to keep your assets offline. Deep cold storage solutions, such as vaults, can be considered for those seeking an even higher level of security. These methods involve storing your keys in highly secure environments, like buried hardware or third-party vault services, ensuring they are protected and difficult to access without deliberate effort.

Setting up a cold storage solution requires careful attention to detail. Begin by protecting your private keys using a secure, offline device. This process ensures that your keys are never exposed to the internet, preventing any potential interception by hackers. Once generated, secure your private keys using your chosen cold storage method. If using a hardware wallet, follow the manufacturer's instructions for setting it up. It typically involves connecting the device to your computer to initialize it. Print your keys on durable, water-resistant paper for paper wallets, and store them safely. Regardless of the method, always create multiple backups of your private keys, storing them in different locations to safeguard against loss or damage.

The benefits of cold storage extend beyond mere security. By keeping your assets offline, you gain immunity to online hacks, a constant threat in cryptocurrency. This added layer of protection provides peace of mind, allowing you to focus on your investment strategy without worrying about the safety of your assets. Cold storage is particularly advantageous for long-term investors, enabling you to securely store large amounts of cryptocurrency without frequent access. This approach mitigates the risks associated with digital theft. It helps cultivate a disciplined investment mindset, encouraging you to hold on to your assets for the long haul.

In the end, cold storage solutions offer a level of security unmatched by any other method. By taking your assets offline, you create a fortress that shields your digital wealth from the perils of the online world. Whether you choose a hardware wallet, a paper wallet, or a more elaborate cold storage method, the key ensures your private keys remain safe and secure. As you navigate cryptocurrency, remember that protecting your assets is paramount. Cold storage provides the peace of mind to explore and engage confidently with exciting opportunities in digital currencies.

Reporting and Recovering from Crypto Fraud

Encountering crypto fraud can feel overwhelming, but taking swift and informed action can make a significant difference. The initial step involves contacting your local authorities. Reporting the incident not only potentially helps to recover your assets, but also aids in building a case against the perpetrators. Local law enforcement agencies are increasingly familiar with cryptocurrency-related crimes and can guide the next steps. Following this, reporting the fraud to regulatory bodies overseeing financial activities is crucial. In the United States, for instance, the Federal Trade Commission (FTC) and the Commodity Futures Trading Commission (CFTC) are pivotal in handling such cases. These organizations collect data on fraudulent activities, which can help identify broader patterns and prevent future scams. You contribute significantly to combating fraud and protecting other potential victims by reporting your case.

The possibility of recovering lost assets varies, depending on the nature of the fraud and the mechanisms in place. Legal action can sometimes lead to restitution, especially if the perpetrators are apprehended and the assets seized. However, this process can be lengthy and complex, with no guaranteed outcomes. Victims may sometimes join class-action lawsuits, which pool resources to build a stronger case. This collective approach can increase the chances of recovery but also requires patience and perseverance. It's essential to manage expectations and understand the limitations of legal avenues. While some individuals have successfully reclaimed their assets, others may only receive partial restitution or none.

Forensic investigation plays a key role in tracing and recovering stolen assets. Blockchain analysis techniques enable investigators to track the movement of cryptocurrencies across the blockchain. These techniques, often employed by specialized firms, can identify wallets associated with fraudulent activities and potentially lead to the recovery of funds. Forensic experts analyze patterns, trace transactions, and work to uncover the identities behind anonymous wallets. This meticulous work requires time and expertise but can yield results, especially with law enforcement efforts. While initially daunting, blockchain technology's transparency can become an asset in uncovering fraudulent schemes and deterring future criminals.

Preventing future fraud involves learning from experiences and implementing stronger defenses. Regularly updating your knowledge about current scams and security practices is vital. Stay informed by following reputable crypto news sources and participating in community discussions. This ongoing education helps you recognize new threats and adapt your strategies accordingly. Reflect on past incidents, identifying what security measures were lacking and how to implement them. Strengthening your defenses might include adopting advanced security tools, diversifying storage methods, and maintaining a skeptical mindset toward unsolicited offers. By taking a proactive stance, you reduce the likelihood of falling victim to fraud again.

In wrapping up this chapter, it's crucial to emphasize that staying alert and making well-informed decisions are paramount in safeguarding against cryptocurrency fraud. Equipping yourself with the proper knowledge and employing effective strategies will empower you to navigate the complex terrain of crypto trading with confidence and security. By remaining vigilant and informed, you position yourself to avoid potential pitfalls and capitalize on the opportunities this dynamic and evolving space offers.

Chapter Six

The Regulatory Landscape

You are at a bustling international airport where passengers from all corners of the globe converge. Each traveler must navigate unique customs and regulations, some welcoming and straightforward, others complex and restrictive. The world of cryptocurrency regulation is much like this airport, where countries adopt varied approaches to managing digital currencies. In Japan, a pioneer in the crypto realm, the government has established a licensing system for exchanges, fostering a secure environment that encourages innovation and investment. This proactive stance has positioned Japan as a leader in the crypto industry, drawing entrepreneurs and investors eager to explore the potential of digital assets.

Conversely, China presents a stark contrast with its stringent ban on cryptocurrency trading. The Chinese government cites concerns over financial stability and capital flight for its restrictive policies. This ban has forced many crypto enthusiasts and businesses to relocate or pivot their operations, highlighting how regulations can dramatically influence market accessibility. In the United States, the approach is more nuanced. The Securities and Exchange Commission (SEC) plays a pivotal role in shaping the crypto landscape, applying existing securities laws to digital assets. The SEC's guidelines focus on protecting investors by classifying many cryptocurrencies as securities, subjecting them to rigorous standards. Meanwhile, the European Union's Markets in Crypto-Assets (MiCA) framework seeks to create a unified regulatory environment across member states, emphasizing transparency and consumer protection. These guidelines aim to harmonize rules and foster a stable market, minimizing risks associated with volatile digital assets.

The reasons behind such diverse regulatory stances are deeply rooted in each nation's economic priorities and risk tolerance. For many countries, ensuring national financial stability remains a top priority. Regulators strive to balance fostering innovation with maintaining control over monetary systems. In some regions, like the EU, consumer protection goals drive regulatory efforts, aiming to shield citizens from fraud and financial loss. These motivations often result in different regulatory stringency levels, reflecting each jurisdiction's unique economic and cultural landscapes.

Examining regulatory challenges and successes provides valuable insights into the complex dynamics of cryptocurrency oversight. Switzerland serves as a notable example of a crypto-friendly regulatory environment. Known for its supportive policies and legal clarity, Switzerland attracts blockchain companies and investors seeking a stable and predictable landscape. The Swiss approach emphasizes clear guidelines and cooperation between regulators and industry participants, fostering an ecosystem conducive to growth and innovation. In contrast, India exemplifies a more turbulent regulatory journey. The country's stance on cryptocurrencies has fluctuated, oscillating between bans and potential regulation. These uncertainties have created challenges for businesses and investors, illustrating the impact of regulatory instability on market development.

Understanding these global regulatory differences is crucial for anyone navigating the cryptocurrency market. As digital assets continue to gain traction, the need for robust and consistent regulations becomes increasingly evident. The ever-evolving landscape of crypto regulation offers opportunities and challenges, profoundly shaping digital currencies' future. Staying informed about regulatory developments is not just a suggestion, it's a necessity. It empowers you to make informed decisions and seize opportunities in this dynamic sector, ensuring you can navigate it effectively.

What You Need to Know about Taxation and Crypto

Understanding how taxes apply to your transactions is crucial in cryptocurrency. Like traditional investments, cryptocurrencies are subject to taxation, primarily around capital gains and income. A taxable event occurs whenever you trade, sell, or earn interest from your digital assets. Therefore, you'll need to pay taxes on the profits you make. For instance, if you buy Bitcoin at a low price and sell it for more later, the profit is taxable as a capital gain. Similarly, if you earn interest from staking or lending your crypto, this income is also subject to taxation. To comply with these requirements, you must accurately calculate your cost basis—the original value of your asset—alongside any gains or losses you experience. For accurate reporting, you'll need to keep detailed records of each transaction, which can be a complex task given the volatile nature of the crypto market.

Ensuring compliance with crypto tax regulations presents several challenges. One significant issue is the difficulty in tracking the history of your transactions, especially if you trade on multiple platforms or use several wallets. Each transaction must be recorded, including the date, amount, and value at the exchange time. This level of detail is necessary to determine your tax liability accurately. Another complexity arises from valuing your digital assets, as cryptocurrency prices fluctuate wildly in short periods. This volatility can complicate calculating gains and losses, as the value of an asset might change significantly between the time you acquire and dispose of it. These factors make it essential to stay organized and up-to-date with your records, ensuring you can meet your tax obligations without unnecessary stress. You can feel responsible and in control of your tax obligations by maintaining accurate records.

Adopting specific strategies can be highly beneficial to maintain accurate records for tax purposes. Utilizing crypto tax software is one practical approach. These tools can automatically track transactions across different platforms, helping you compile the necessary information with minimal effort. They can also assist in calculating your capital gains and losses, making it easier to report your crypto activities on your tax return. Documenting transaction details is another crucial step. Keep records of every purchase, sale, and trade, noting the date, amount, and value in your local currency. This comprehensive documentation will be invaluable if you ever face an audit or need to verify your tax filings. By staying diligent and organized, you can confidently and easily navigate the complexities of crypto taxation.

Exploring potential tax strategies can offer significant advantages for crypto investors looking to optimize their tax obligations. One such approach is tax-loss harvesting, which involves selling assets that have lost value to offset gains from more profitable investments. This strategy can help reduce your overall tax liability, providing a valuable tool in your financial planning arsenal. Additionally, understanding the importance of holding periods is crucial. In many jurisdictions, having an asset for more than a year can qualify you for long-term capital gains tax rates, typically lower than short-term rates. By strategically timing your trades and holding assets for the appropriate duration, you can minimize your tax burden and maximize your after-tax returns. These strategies can give you a sense of control and optimism in managing your tax obligations.

Navigating the intricacies of cryptocurrency taxation is an essential step for any investor looking to remain on the right side of tax regulations while maximizing their financial gains. It's crucial to gain an in-depth understanding of the fundamental principles and strategic approaches to handling your crypto assets from a tax perspective. This involves staying up-to-date with the latest tax laws and guidelines that pertain to cryptocurrency, identifying taxable events within your crypto activities, and employing strategies to optimize your tax obligations. By doing so, you not only ensure compliance with the relevant tax laws but also position yourself to enhance your financial outcomes through informed decision-making and strategic planning.

Navigating Compliance: Staying on the Right Side of the Law

In cryptocurrency, staying compliant with regulations is as crucial as keeping your car in good working order. Non-compliance can lead to hefty fines and legal repercussions that could derail your financial plans. Consider the penalties for non-reporting of crypto transactions. Like failing to declare income on your tax return, neglecting to report crypto gains or losses could result in significant financial penalties. Moreover, engaging in illicit activities such as money laundering through digital currencies invites legal action. It can tarnish your reputation, making it harder to participate in legitimate markets in the future.

Understanding your local crypto regulations is analogous to knowing the rules of the road before you drive. Each jurisdiction has its laws governing cryptocurrencies, which can vary widely. To ensure you're on the right side of the law, visit government websites that often provide invaluable resources and updates on regulatory changes. These sites can offer insights into requirements for compliance in your area. Additionally, consulting legal experts specializing in cryptocurrency can provide tailored advice. They can help interpret complex legal jargon and ensure you're fully aware of your legal obligations. This proactive approach safeguards your investments and instills confidence as you navigate the crypto landscape.

Compliance tools and services act as your co-pilot, helping maintain your course. Compliance software solutions are beneficial for those trading across multiple platforms or jurisdictions. These programs can track transactions, flag potential compliance issues, and help generate reports needed for regulatory purposes. They are like having an accountant specializing in crypto, ensuring all your data is accurate and up-to-date. For more personalized assistance, consider professional advisory services. These experts can provide strategic insights and help develop a compliance framework tailored to your needs. Whether you're a casual investor or run a crypto-based business, these tools and services can be invaluable in maintaining regulatory compliance.

Adapting to regulatory changes is like adjusting your sails to the wind. The crypto regulatory landscape continually evolves, and staying informed is key to remaining compliant. One effective strategy is subscribing to regulatory newsletters that provide updates on changes in laws and regulations. These newsletters often include expert analysis and are an excellent way to keep abreast of developments that might affect your investments. Participating in industry forums and discussions is another way to stay informed. These platforms allow you to engage with other investors, share insights, and gain different perspectives on how regulations impact the market. By actively participating in these communities, you can better anticipate changes and adapt your strategies accordingly.

Compliance Checklist

Establish a comprehensive checklist of compliance tasks to ensure you remain within legal boundaries while engaging in cryptocurrency trading. This list should include regular actions such as:Monthly review of local and international cryptocurrency regulations to stay abreast of any changes that could affect your trading activities.

- Quarterly consultations with a legal expert specializing in cryptocurrency. This professional can provide personalized advice and insights on navigating the legal landscape and ensuring your trading practices are compliant.

- Annual audits of your cryptocurrency transactions and holdings. This practice helps maintain transparency and can be beneficial for tax purposes and in the event of any legal scrutiny.

- Setting up alerts for news on cryptocurrency legislation through reliable financial news sources.

This proactive approach keeps you informed of real-time updates and potential shifts in the regulatory environment. Incorporating these tasks into your routine creates a structured approach to compliance, safeguarding your investments against legal complications and penalties.

The Role of Governments and Central Banks in Crypto

Governments worldwide have varied perspectives on cryptocurrencies, often reflecting a balance between seeing digital currencies as opportunities and threats. On one hand, cryptocurrencies represent economic opportunities by fostering innovation, attracting investment, and enhancing the efficiency of financial transactions. They can spur job creation in tech sectors and provide new avenues for economic growth. On the other hand, they threaten traditional financial systems, particularly concerning the sovereignty of national currencies. As decentralized currencies, cryptocurrencies challenge governments' control over monetary policy, raising concerns about their impact on financial stability and the effectiveness of economic interventions. This competition with sovereign currencies is critical, prompting governments to tread carefully in their regulatory approaches.

Central banks play a pivotal role in shaping digital currency policies, with many exploring the development of Central Bank Digital Currencies (CBDCs). These government-backed digital currencies complement or replace physical cash, offering a secure and regulated alternative to private cryptocurrencies. CBDCs aim to harness the benefits of digital currency while maintaining the stability and trust inherent in traditional fiat currencies. The creation of CBDCs also has significant implications for monetary policy, as they could provide central banks with new tools to manage economic fluctuations. For example, CBDCs could facilitate more targeted monetary interventions, such as direct transfers to citizens during economic downturns, thereby enhancing the effectiveness of fiscal policy. As a result, central banks are increasingly involved in the digital currency landscape, shaping the future of money.

The challenge for governments lies in balancing innovation with control. Encouraging technological advancement while maintaining regulatory oversight is a delicate task. Regulatory sandboxes offer a promising solution, allowing companies to test new financial products and services in a controlled environment. These sandboxes provide a framework for innovation, enabling regulators to monitor developments closely and assess potential risks. Public-private partnerships are another avenue for fostering collaboration between governments and the crypto industry. By working together, these entities can develop regulatory frameworks that protect consumers while promoting growth and innovation. This balance is crucial for realizing the benefits of digital currencies without compromising financial stability or security.

Several countries have taken proactive steps to embrace and regulate cryptocurrencies. Estonia, for instance, has implemented an e-residency program that allows entrepreneurs to establish and manage businesses online, regardless of their physical location. This initiative leverages blockchain technology to streamline administrative processes, making it easier for digital nomads and international business owners to operate globally. Estonia's approach demonstrates how governments can harness the potential of digital currencies to enhance economic competitiveness and attract global talent. Similarly, Singapore has developed a comprehensive regulatory framework supporting its fintech sector's growth. The Monetary Authority of Singapore (MAS) has established clear guidelines for cryptocurrency exchanges and service providers, fostering an environment conducive to innovation while ensuring robust consumer protection. Singapore's regulatory framework highlights the importance of clarity and consistency in fostering a thriving crypto ecosystem.

Understanding KYC and AML in Crypto Trading

Imagine entering a secure bank vault, where every transaction and identity is meticulously verified. This verification is the essence of Know Your Customer (KYC) in the cryptocurrency ecosystem. KYC requirements are crucial for maintaining trust and integrity, ensuring users are who they claim to be. At the heart of KYC is identity verification, which involves collecting personal information, such as government-issued identification, proof of address, and sometimes even a selfie for facial recognition. This documentation is necessary to create a clear identity profile, reducing the risk of fraud and allowing platforms to comply with legal requirements. By verifying identities, exchanges can better protect against illicit activities and provide a safe environment for trading. While seemingly intrusive, submitting these documents forms the backbone of a secure trading experience, safeguarding both users and the platform.

Equally important are Anti-Money Laundering (AML) regulations, which are a bulwark against using cryptocurrencies for illegal purposes. AML laws play a critical role in monitoring and preventing suspicious transactions, a task made challenging by the pseudonymous nature of digital currencies. Exchanges are required to implement robust systems to detect and report unusual activities, such as large or irregular transactions that might indicate money laundering or other criminal activities. This obligation extends to maintaining detailed records of all transactions, enabling authorities to trace and investigate potential illicit activities. By enforcing these standards, AML regulations help ensure that the cryptocurrency market remains a legitimate and trustworthy space for investors and traders.

To illustrate the practical application of KYC and AML regulations, consider how significant exchanges like Coinbase and Binance operate. Coinbase, for example, requires users to verify their identity before engaging in any transactions. This process involves uploading identification documents and undergoing a verification check, which can take a few minutes to a couple of days, depending on the volume of requests. Binance, on the other hand, employs advanced monitoring systems to track transaction patterns and flag any anomalies that might suggest fraudulent activity. These platforms demonstrate the importance of adhering to KYC and AML requirements, showcasing how they contribute to a secure trading environment.

For traders, ensuring compliance with KYC and AML requirements is vital. Start by preparing the necessary documentation before you begin trading. Items needed typically include a government-issued ID, proof of residence, and any additional documents the platform might require. Understanding the specific policies of the exchange you're using is also crucial. Each platform may have different requirements or processes, so familiarize yourself with these details to avoid delays or issues. By staying informed and proactive, you can easily navigate the complexities of KYC and AML, ensuring that your trading activities remain compliant and secure.

What to Expect in Future Regulatory Trends

A significant evolution in the regulatory landscape for cryptocurrencies will take place. One area likely to see increased scrutiny is stablecoins. These digital assets, pegged to traditional currencies like the US dollar, offer a bridge between the volatile world of cryptocurrencies and the stability of fiat money. However, their rapid growth and widespread use have raised concerns among regulators about their potential impact on financial stability. Expect future regulations to focus on ensuring that stablecoin issuers maintain adequate reserves and transparency, akin to traditional banking standards. This increased oversight aims to safeguard users and maintain trust in these hybrid financial instruments.

In parallel, we may witness the emergence of global regulatory standards for cryptocurrencies. As digital currencies transcend borders, the need for a unified approach becomes more apparent. Initiatives by global regulatory bodies, such as the Financial Stability Board and the International Monetary Fund, are working towards establishing consistent guidelines. These efforts aim to harmonize regulations across countries, reducing regulatory arbitrage where entities could exploit differing rules between jurisdictions. By aligning international standards, regulators hope to foster a safer and more predictable environment for crypto markets, enhancing investor confidence and market integrity.

Technological advancements will also shape future regulations. Blockchain analytics tools, for instance, are becoming more sophisticated, offering regulators enhanced capabilities to monitor transactions and detect illicit activities. These tools provide a clearer view of the blockchain's vast data landscape, enabling more effective enforcement of compliance measures. Similarly, decentralized finance (DeFi) innovations present new regulatory challenges and opportunities. DeFi platforms operate without traditional intermediaries, offering financial services through smart contracts. While this innovation promotes financial inclusivity, it raises questions about oversight and consumer protection. Regulators may need to develop novel approaches to address the unique risks and benefits associated with DeFi, ensuring that these platforms operate transparently and safely.

International cooperation will be vital in shaping the future of crypto regulation. Bilateral agreements between countries can facilitate information sharing and best practices, strengthening efforts to combat cross-border financial crimes. Additionally, collaborative initiatives by global regulatory bodies can provide a framework for addressing common challenges, such as money laundering and fraud. Countries can create a cohesive regulatory environment that supports innovation while mitigating risks by working together. This cooperative approach is crucial in a digital landscape where borders are increasingly blurred, and one nation's actions can have far-reaching implications.

Insights from industry experts shed light on the future trajectory of crypto regulation. Regulatory professionals emphasize the importance of balancing innovation with consumer protection. They advocate for a flexible regulatory framework that can adapt to the rapid pace of technological change. Crypto industry leaders echo these sentiments, highlighting the need for clarity and consistency in regulations. They argue that clear guidelines can reduce uncertainty and encourage more widespread adoption of digital currencies. As we move forward, these expert perspectives will play a pivotal role in shaping policies that support the growth and maturation of the crypto ecosystem.

In summary, the future of cryptocurrency regulation promises to be dynamic and multifaceted. With increased focus on stablecoins, the potential for global standards, and the influence of emerging technologies, the regulatory landscape will continue to evolve. International cooperation and expert insights will guide this evolution, ensuring regulations keep pace with innovation while safeguarding users and the broader financial system. This chapter has explored the complexities of crypto regulation, setting the stage for a more in-depth understanding of how these digital assets are reshaping our world. As we transition to the next chapter, we will delve into building wealth with cryptocurrency, exploring strategies and opportunities in this ever-changing space.

Chapter Seven

Building Wealth with Cryptocurrency

N ow you are standing on the edge of a vast digital frontier, where innovation and opportunity intertwine to reshape the very fabric of finance. This scene vividly describes the world of cryptocurrency—a realm brimming with potential for those ready to explore. Integrating artificial intelligence into blockchain technology has recently opened new avenues for growth. AI can enhance blockchain efficiency by automating complex processes and improving decision-making through data analysis. For instance, AI-driven crypto trading bots can analyze vast market data, executing trades with precision and speed surpassing human capabilities. As these technologies converge, they offer groundbreaking investment opportunities, potentially transforming industries from logistics to healthcare by optimizing operations and unlocking new efficiencies.

Alongside AI, developing Layer 2 scaling solutions addresses one of the most pressing challenges in the crypto space: scalability. As more people use cryptocurrencies, the systems can get clogged up, leading to slow transactions and high fees. Layer 2 solutions, like the Lightning Network for Bitcoin, aim to fix this by processing transactions differently, which speeds things up and makes them cheaper. This innovation makes using cryptocurrencies easier and cheaper, which could encourage more people to use them. As these technologies improve, they promise to make the financial system work more smoothly and efficiently.

The path forward is not without obstacles. Regulatory hurdles loom large over the cryptocurrency landscape as governments grapple with how to govern this rapidly growing sector. Regulatory clarity is crucial for fostering innovation and protecting consumers, yet the lack of uniform policies across regions creates uncertainty. This inconsistency can stifle growth as businesses navigate a patchwork of rules. Moreover, the environmental impact of cryptocurrency mining, particularly for proof-of-work currencies like Bitcoin, raises concerns. The substantial energy consumption associated with mining—often reliant on fossil fuels—has sparked debates about sustainability. Addressing these environmental issues is vital for ensuring the long-term viability of cryptocurrencies and aligning with global efforts to combat climate change.

Institutional investment plays a pivotal role in shaping the future of cryptocurrencies. The entry of major financial institutions into the crypto space signifies a shift from skepticism to acceptance. Institutional investors bring capital, credibility, and an expectation of stability, which can enhance market liquidity and reduce volatility. Their involvement legitimizes cryptocurrencies as a viable asset class, attracting more participants and fostering innovation. For instance, the approval of Bitcoin ETFs by regulatory bodies has opened the floodgates for institutional investment, driving significant capital into the market. This influx has the potential to stabilize prices and increase adoption as digital assets integrate more deeply with traditional finance.

In the future, several scenarios could define the trajectory of the cryptocurrency landscape. Increased global adoption is one possibility as more individuals and businesses realize the benefits of digital currencies. Such recognition could lead to widespread acceptance in everyday transactions, further integrating crypto into the fabric of global commerce. Technological breakthroughs, such as advancements in quantum computing or novel consensus algorithms, may also reshape the field, introducing new capabilities and efficiencies. However, these developments come with risks, including potential security threats and the need for ongoing adaptation to regulatory changes. Navigating this evolving landscape requires vigilance and a willingness to embrace change as opportunities and challenges abound in the quest for financial growth and innovation.

Visualizing the Crypto Future

- To deepen your understanding of cryptocurrency's future, creating a mind map that lays out its potential growth scenarios alongside the challenges it may encounter is beneficial

- Start by pinpointing key trends that are shaping the cryptocurrency world. For instance, integrating Artificial Intelligence (AI) and developing Layer 2 scaling solutions are significant.

- AI integration uses machine learning and other AI technologies to improve cryptocurrency platforms' functionality, security, and user experience.

- On the other hand, Layer 2 scaling solutions are technologies built on top of existing blockchain networks to increase their transaction processing capabilities, making them faster and more efficient.

- Once these trends are identified, connect them to possible outcomes they could lead to. For example, the successful integration of AI could result in more secure and user-friendly platforms, potentially leading to increased cryptocurrency adoption by the general public

- Similarly, effective Layer 2 solutions could solve some of the scalability issues of popular cryptocurrencies, making them more practical for everyday transactions and thereby contributing to their wider adoption. However, linking these trends to potential challenges, such as regulatory hurdles, is crucial.

As cryptocurrencies become more integrated into mainstream financial systems, they are likely to attract more attention from regulatory bodies, which could lead to stricter regulations. This could impact how cryptocurrencies operate and how they are adopted across different markets. Reflecting on these scenarios can provide valuable insights into how the cryptocurrency landscape might evolve and influence your investment strategy. By understanding both the potential growth areas and the challenges, you can make more informed decisions about navigating the crypto space, diversifying your portfolio, and potentially building wealth with cryptocurrency investments. This approach allows you to not only appreciate the complexity of the market but also to strategize effectively in the face of uncertainty.

What Beginners Should Know About Investing in ICOs

Think of Initial Coin Offerings, or ICOs, as the digital age's answer to traditional Initial Public Offerings (IPOs). Both serve as methods for raising capital, yet they operate in different arenas. While IPOs offer shares of a company to the public, ICOs present a new cryptocurrency or token to potential investors. These tokens often represent a stake in a project or grant access to a specific service or product. For startups and new ventures in the crypto space, ICOs provide a quicker, less regulated avenue to gather funds compared to the often cumbersome and regulated process of IPOs. For early investors, ICOs can offer the tantalizing prospect of acquiring tokens at a bargain price, hoping their value will soar as the project gains traction.

Yet, the allure of ICOs comes with its risks and rewards. On one hand, the potential for substantial returns is undeniable. Early backers of successful ICOs have witnessed their investments multiply, sometimes exponentially, as the projects they supported succeed. However, the landscape is fraught with challenges. The absence of stringent regulation means ICOs are susceptible to fraud and failure. Scammers are known to exploit the excitement around ICOs, launching projects with little intention of following through. Even legitimate projects can falter, as the volatile nature of the crypto market and unforeseen technical hurdles can impede progress. Thus, investing in ICOs requires careful balancing of risk and reward, with due diligence paramount. When considering an ICO investment, knowing these risks and rewards is essential.

To navigate the ICO landscape effectively, a robust framework for evaluation is crucial. Start by examining the project's whitepaper, a document outlining its vision, technology, and roadmap. A well-crafted whitepaper should clearly understand the project's feasibility and potential for success. Pay close attention to the problem the project aims to solve, the proposed solution, and the underlying technology. Equally important is the team behind the project. Investigate their backgrounds and track records. A team with proven experience and expertise in relevant fields can strongly indicate a project's potential success. Look for transparency in communication and a genuine commitment to the project's goals.

In the world of ICOs, diversification is a prudent strategy. As one wouldn't invest all their savings into a single stock, spreading investments across multiple ICOs can mitigate risk. Doing so increases the chances of backing a successful project while minimizing potential losses from those who fail. It is also wise to keep a finger on the pulse of industry trends. Staying informed about emerging technologies and market shifts can help identify promising ICOs with the potential for long-term success. Engage with online communities, read industry reports, and follow thought leaders to gain insights into which projects are gaining traction and why.

ICO Evaluation Checklist

Creating a Checklist for Evaluating ICO Projects to navigate the landscape of Initial Coin Offerings (ICOs) effectively and developing a meticulous checklist is paramount. This checklist will serve as your compass, guiding you through many projects vying for your investment. Here are the critical criteria to include in your evaluation process:

- **Whitepaper Clarity and Completeness**: A project's whitepaper is its blueprint. It should clearly outline its goals, technology, roadmap, and how to address existing market problems. A well-articulated whitepaper indicates a project's seriousness and potential for success.

- **Team Credentials and Experience**: The team behind an ICO is as crucial as the project itself. Research the team members' backgrounds, experience in blockchain technology, and track record in other ventures. A strong, experienced team increases the likelihood of the project's success.

- **Technological Innovation and Solution**: Evaluate the uniqueness and necessity of the ICO proposed technology. Does it offer a genuine solution to a real problem? Is the technology behind it innovative, or just replicating existing solutions? Projects that bring novel solutions to pressing issues are more likely to thrive.

- **Community Engagement and Support**: A vibrant, engaged community is a positive indicator of an ICO's health and potential. Active engagement on social media, forums, and other platforms can provide insights into the project's reception and the team's commitment to transparency and communication.

- **Tokenomics and Use Case**: Understand the token's utility within the project. Does it have a clear use case that supports the project's ecosystem? Evaluate the token distribution plan, total supply, and how the funds raised will be used. A well-thought-out tokenomics model can ensure the project's long-term viability.

- **Regulatory Compliance**: Ensure the ICO complies with relevant legal and regulatory requirements. Non-compliance can lead to project shutdowns and investment loss.

- **Market Potential and Competition**: Assess the project's market and competition potential. A project addressing a sizable market with limited competition might offer better growth prospects. By applying this checklist to assess potential ICO investments, you can systematically identify opportunities with a higher likelihood of success and mitigate the risks associated with trading in this volatile market.

Generating Passive Income from Yield Farming and Staking

In cryptocurrency, yield farming and staking have become two popular methods for investors to earn passive income. These strategies allow you to put your digital assets to work, generating returns without actively trading them. Yield farming provides liquidity to decentralized finance (DeFi) platforms, facilitating trading, lending, and borrowing without traditional intermediaries. Depositing your cryptocurrency into a liquidity pool enables others to use these funds for transactions. In return, you earn a share of the transaction fees or interest, often paid in the platform's native token. This approach capitalizes on your existing holdings, like earning dividends from stocks or interest from a savings account, turning idle assets into income-generating tools.

Staking involves holding cryptocurrencies in a wallet to support the operations of a blockchain network. In proof-of-stake (PoS) systems, staking is essential for network security and transaction validation. By locking up your coins, you help maintain the network, and in return, your assets earn staking rewards. Some networks employ delegated proof-of-stake (DPoS), where you can delegate your tokens to a validator who performs the network's tasks on your behalf. Platforms like Cardano and Polkadot exemplify successful staking environments, offering participants steady rewards. This process supports the network and provides a passive income stream akin to earning interest on a fixed deposit.

While yield farming and staking offer attractive returns, they carry inherent risks. Yield farming can yield high interest rates, sometimes reaching double digits annually. However, accompanied by these gains is the risk of smart contract vulnerabilities. DeFi platforms rely on complex code, and any flaws can lead to significant financial losses. In addition, the volatile nature of cryptocurrency prices can alter the value of your rewards, particularly if paid in a token that loses value. Staking is generally considered less risky, but it has challenges. The value of the staked coin can fluctuate, affecting your overall returns. Moreover, some networks impose lock-up periods, during which your funds are inaccessible, potentially missing out on other investment opportunities.

Select a suitable DeFi platform known for its security and reputation for yield farming—research platforms like Uniswap or Aave offer user-friendly interfaces and robust security measures. Once you've chosen a platform, you'll need to understand the dynamics of liquidity pools. These pools consist of token pairs, such as ETH/DAI, where you provide equal value for both tokens. Your share of the pool determines your share of the fees generated. Monitoring pool performance and market conditions is crucial, as these can influence your earnings. Regularly review your investments and consider diversifying across multiple pools to mitigate risk.

Staking, by contrast, is often more straightforward to initiate. Select a cryptocurrency that supports staking, such as Cardano or Polkadot. Create a wallet compatible with staking, and transfer your tokens into it. Next, choose a validator or staking pool to delegate your tokens. This choice is critical, as the validator's performance affects your rewards. Look for validators with a strong track record and low commission fees. Once you've delegated your tokens, you can sit back and earn rewards, typically distributed at regular intervals. Monitoring your stake and validator performance ensures you maximize your returns and adjust as necessary.

Expanding Your Financial Horizons by Leveraging DeFi

Consider a world where financial services are accessible to anyone with an internet connection, bypassing traditional banks and intermediaries. Such a reality is the promise of decentralized finance, or DeFi. By eliminating the intermediaries, DeFi opens the door to a more inclusive financial system, offering a lifeline to the unbanked and underbanked populations globally. It's a revolutionary shift where digital platforms replace brick-and-mortar banks, allowing you to engage in lending, borrowing, and trading with a few clicks. The potential for DeFi to transform traditional finance lies in its decentralized nature, where smart contracts—self-executing agreements coded on blockchain technology—ensure transparency and security.

The appeal of DeFi lies in its diverse applications, which mirror yet enhance conventional financial services. Decentralized lending and borrowing platforms like Aave allow users to lend their cryptocurrency and earn interest. At the same time, borrowers can access funds without the lengthy approval processes typical of banks. These platforms operate round-the-clock, offering flexibility and access to capital when needed. Decentralized exchanges (DEXs) such as Uniswap and SushiSwap provide another facet for DeFi. Unlike traditional exchanges, DEXs facilitate peer-to-peer trading without an intermediary, giving users greater control and privacy over their transactions. These platforms utilize liquidity pools, where users contribute assets to facilitate trades, earning a portion of the trading fees in return.

Yet, while DeFi presents enticing opportunities, it is not without its risks. High-yield opportunities often come with increased exposure to volatility and security vulnerabilities. DeFi platforms, reliant on complex smart contracts, are occasionally susceptible to hacks and exploits. In 2022 alone, over $3 billion was lost to DeFi hacks, highlighting the importance of diligence and security measures. These incidents underscore the critical need for thorough research into DeFi projects before participation. Evaluating a platform's security protocols, auditing history, and community reputation can provide insights into its reliability. Additionally, market volatility impacts the value of assets staked or lent on these platforms, necessitating careful consideration of risk tolerance before engaging.

Safely navigating the DeFi landscape requires a strategic approach. Conducting comprehensive research into DeFi projects is paramount. Scrutinize the project's whitepaper, audit reports, and community discussions to gauge its credibility and potential. Look for teams with strong track records and transparency in operations. Diversifying your investments across multiple DeFi projects can mitigate risks. Just as you wouldn't invest all your savings into a single stock, spreading your capital across different platforms reduces the impact of any one project's failure. In addition, keeping informed about the latest developments in DeFi can help you adapt to changes and seize new opportunities. Engaging with online forums and following industry leaders can provide valuable insights into emerging trends.

DeFi Risk Assessment Checklist

To enhance your decision-making process when exploring DeFi (Decentralized Finance) investments, it's wise to develop a comprehensive risk assessment checklist. This checklist should encompass several critical criteria to meticulously evaluate the safety and potential of the platforms you're considering. Key elements to include are:

- **Project's Security Audits**: Look for detailed security audits from reputable firms. These audits assess the project's smart contracts and overall security architecture, identifying vulnerabilities that attackers could exploit. A project with regular and recent security audits demonstrates a commitment to safeguarding users' assets.

- **Team's Credibility**: Investigate the track record and transparency of the project's founding and current team members. A credible team will have a history of successful projects and a transparent, verifiable professional background. Trustworthy projects often have well-known team members in the crypto community and openly communicate with users.

- **Community Feedback**: Gauge the sentiment and feedback from the project's user community. Communities can be found on social media platforms, forums, and the project's official communication channels. Positive feedback, active user engagement, and responsive support from the project team are good indicators of a healthy ecosystem.

- **Smart Contract Transparency**: Ensure the project's smart contracts are open source and publicly available for review. Transparency in smart contracts allows for independent verification of the code's integrity and functionality, reducing the risk of hidden malicious code or backdoors.

Incorporating these criteria into your DeFi investment risk assessment checklist will provide a structured platform evaluation approach. This methodical evaluation will assist you in making more informed decisions, ultimately helping to protect your investments in the fast-evolving landscape of decentralized finance.

Finding Your Balance Between Long-Term vs. Short-Term Investments

Navigating the world of investments feels like choosing between a marathon and a sprint. Long-term and short-term strategies offer unique paths to financial growth, shaped by distinct characteristics and objectives. Long-term investments focus on wealth accumulation over extended periods, capitalizing on the power of compounding and market growth. This approach aligns with goals such as retirement savings or funding future education, where the emphasis is on steady growth rather than immediate returns. Investors in this category often select stable assets, like blue-chip stocks or established cryptocurrencies, allowing time to weather market fluctuations and benefit from gradual appreciation.

In contrast, short-term investments aim for quick profits, capitalizing on market volatility and rapid price changes. Active traders in this domain might engage in day or swing trading, buying and selling assets within days or hours to capture swift gains. This strategy requires you to keep an eye on market trends and a willingness to take calculated risks, as the potential for significant returns comes with heightened exposure to loss. Short-term investments often suit individuals seeking to boost their income or test new trading techniques. Still, they demand vigilance and a readiness to respond to sudden market shifts.

Choosing the right investment strategy hinges on your financial goals and risk tolerance. Begin by assessing what you hope to achieve financially, whether building a nest egg for the future or generating additional income. Consider your comfort level with risk and how much time you can dedicate to managing your investments. Evaluating current market conditions also plays a role. Short-term strategies yield higher rewards in a bullish market with rising prices. In contrast, a bearish market could favor the stability of long-term holdings. Aligning your strategy with these factors ensures your investments fit your unique situation and aspirations.

A balanced approach to investing combines the strengths of both long-term and short-term strategies, offering a diversified portfolio that mitigates risk while maximizing potential gains. This method allows flexibility in adapting to market changes, ensuring you can seize opportunities as they arise without compromising your long-term objectives. For instance, dedicating 70% of your portfolio to long-term holdings provides a stable foundation, supporting sustained growth and financial security. Then, allocate the remaining 30% to short-term trading, where you can explore new markets, capitalize on trends, and enhance your overall returns.

Consider a balanced portfolio as a dynamic blend of stability and agility. A substantial portion might include established assets like Bitcoin or Ethereum, renowned for their resilience and growth potential. These long-term investments serve as the core, providing security and gradual appreciation. Meanwhile, the short-term segment could involve trading emerging tokens or participating in market events like halving cycles, where quick decisions can yield substantial profits. This diversified approach spreads risk across different asset classes and positions you to benefit from various market conditions, ensuring your investments remain robust and adaptable.

Embracing a balanced investment strategy empowers you to confidently find your way through the complexities of the digital finance landscape. By blending long-term and short-term approaches, you create a portfolio that leverages the best of both worlds, combining the security of stable growth with the excitement of potential quick gains. This holistic perspective allows you to respond to market dynamics effectively, ensuring your financial journey is rewarding and resilient. Through careful planning and strategic allocation, you can build a diversified portfolio that supports your goals and adapts to the ever-evolving world of cryptocurrency.

Learning from Successful Crypto Investors

In the ever-evolving landscape of cryptocurrency, learning from those who have navigated its complexities successfully can offer invaluable insights. Renowned crypto investors often emphasize the importance of continuous learning and adaptability. The crypto market is dynamic, with new technologies, regulations, and trends emerging regularly. Staying informed and flexible allows investors to capitalize on opportunities while mitigating risks. This mindset is not just about keeping up with the latest buzz; it's about understanding the underlying mechanisms and being prepared to shift strategies as the market evolves. Successful investors view each market fluctuation as a learning opportunity, refining their approaches and broadening their knowledge base.

Common traits among successful crypto investors include patience and discipline. These individuals understand that the market can be volatile and resist the urge to make impulsive decisions based on short-term price movements. Instead, they maintain a long-term perspective, focusing on their financial goals. Patience allows them to weather market downturns without panic. At the same time, discipline ensures they stick to their strategy, avoiding emotional reactions to market noise. Data-driven decision-making is another hallmark of successful investors. They rely on thorough analysis and empirical evidence rather than speculation or hearsay to guide their investments. By grounding their decisions in data, they reduce the influence of emotions and increase the likelihood of achieving consistent returns.

Early Bitcoin adopters serve as notable examples of successful crypto investors. Those who invested in Bitcoin during its infancy, when it was still a relatively obscure digital asset, reaped substantial rewards as its value surged. Their success was not only due to luck; it was a combination of foresight, conviction, and a willingness to embrace the unknown. Similarly, backers of successful Decentralized Finance (DeFi) projects have seen significant gains. They recognized the potential of DeFi to disrupt traditional financial systems and invested in promising platforms like Aave and Compound. These investors understood the transformative potential of DeFi, and their faith in the technology paid off as these platforms gained traction and value.

To emulate the practices of successful crypto investors, consider setting clear investment goals. Define what you hope to achieve with your investments- long-term wealth accumulation or short-term gains. Having specific goals provides direction and helps you stay focused amidst the market's volatility. Regularly reviewing and adjusting your portfolio is also crucial. The crypto market is not static; your investment strategy should reflect this reality. By periodically assessing your portfolio, you can make informed decisions about when to reallocate assets, take profits, or cut losses. A proactive approach aligns your investments with your evolving financial objectives and market conditions.

Incorporating these strategies into your investment approach can enhance your chances of success. Continuous learning keeps you informed and adaptable, while patience and discipline help you navigate the market's ups and downs. By setting clear goals and regularly reviewing your portfolio, you position yourself to make informed, data-driven decisions. As you engage with the crypto space, remember that success is about making the right investments and cultivating the appropriate mindset and practices.

Chapter Eight

Staying Informed and Engaged

You're navigating a bustling city. The skyline constantly shifts, new skyscrapers emerge overnight, and the map you had yesterday is outdated by morning. This city is the world of cryptocurrency—a dynamic and ever-evolving landscape. Staying informed is not just a choice, but a necessity to thrive and make informed decisions. In the vibrant and rapidly changing cryptocurrency market, staying informed is key to unlocking opportunities and overcoming challenges. You need access to reliable information and diverse perspectives to navigate this world successfully. In this chapter, we will explore how to keep your finger on the pulse of the crypto market and the importance of critical thinking in discerning valuable insights from noise.

Reliable Sources for Crypto News and Analysis

In cryptocurrency, where rumors can spark price swings and misinformation can lead to costly mistakes, identifying trustworthy news outlets is crucial. CoinDesk is among the most reputable sources, offering comprehensive news articles, videos, and newsletters covering the latest crypto developments. CoinDesk has built a reputation for delivering unbiased and accurate information, making it a go-to resource for investors and enthusiasts. Another reliable source is CoinTelegraph, known for its daily updates on market trends, regulatory changes, and technological advancements. CoinTelegraph provides a worldwide perspective on the crypto landscape, helping readers stay informed about key events that could impact their investments. For those seeking in-depth market analysis, The Block is an invaluable resource. It offers research reports and data dashboards that delve into the cryptocurrency market's intricacies, providing insights beyond surface-level news.

While these outlets offer reliable information, consuming news from various perspectives is essential to avoid bias. Traditional financial news sources like Bloomberg can provide a balanced view by covering cryptocurrency alongside other financial markets. This broader context helps you understand how crypto trends fit into the larger economic picture. By diversifying your news sources, you gain a more comprehensive understanding of the market, allowing you to make well-informed decisions. Moreover, engaging with diverse perspectives involves getting different interpretations and analyses and fostering critical thinking. It enables you to question assumptions and form conclusions, enhancing your ability to navigate cryptocurrency.

In an era of information overload, filtering out misinformation is essential. One effective strategy is cross-referencing news with multiple sources. News appearing on several reputable outlets is more likely to be accurate. Fact-checking platforms can also help verify the credibility of the information you encounter. These platforms use rigorous methodologies to assess the accuracy of claims, providing an additional layer of assurance. By adopting a critical mindset and questioning the reliability of information, you can protect yourself from falling victim to misinformation and make more confident investment choices. This critical mindset is a powerful tool as you navigate the cryptocurrency landscape.

Several analysts and influencers have emerged within the crypto community as key figures worth following for their insights. On Crypto Twitter, personalities like Vitalik Buterin, the creator of Ethereum, and Anthony Pompliano, a prominent advocate of Bitcoin, offer valuable perspectives and updates on industry developments. These influencers often share their thoughts on market trends, technological advancements, and policy changes, providing followers with a more in-depth understanding of the crypto ecosystem. Additionally, YouTube channels like Altcoin Daily, run by brothers Aaron and Austin Arnold, offer engaging content and accurate predictions, making them popular crypto news and analysis sources. By following these voices, you'll gain access to a wealth of information and stay connected with the latest happenings in the crypto world.

News Source Evaluation Checklist

Developing a checklist for evaluating news sources is crucial for obtaining reliable information, especially in the fast-evolving world of cryptocurrency. Your checklist should include several key criteria to help you assess the credibility and quality of the information you come across.

- First, consider the reputation of the outlet. Look for news sources that are well-regarded in the cryptocurrency community and have a track record of accuracy and integrity.

- Next, seek out diverse perspectives. A single source may not provide the full picture or have inherent biases. Comparing information from multiple reputable sources can help you better understand the topic.

- Additionally, cross-referencing information with other reputable platforms is essential. If a piece of news is only reported by one source and you can't find any corroboration from other trusted news outlets, it might be a red flag. Reliable news tends to be widely reported by several credible platforms.

By using this checklist to assess the credibility of the news you consume, you'll be better equipped to navigate the complexities of the crypto landscape with confidence and clarity. This approach helps you make informed decisions and safeguard against misinformation and potential scams in the cryptocurrency space.

Realize the Benefits of Networking by Joining Crypto Communities

Finding a community in the vast and sometimes overwhelming cryptocurrency world can feel like discovering a beacon of light. Online forums and groups offer a space to share experiences, exchange knowledge, and find support. These communities become especially valuable as they provide real-time insights and updates on market trends, often before they hit mainstream media. Reddit's cryptocurrency Subreddit, for example, serves as a bustling hub where enthusiasts and experts gather to discuss the latest developments, share technical analyses, and exchange investment strategies. It's a place where you can pose questions and receive answers from diverse perspectives, helping broaden your understanding and refine your approach to investing.

Similarly, Telegram groups focused on specific coins or projects offer another layer of engagement. These groups facilitate direct interaction with developers and project leaders, allowing you to gain firsthand insights into their visions and progress. You can engage in discussions, participate in AMAs (Ask Me Anything sessions), and even contribute ideas that influence the direction of a project. The immediacy of communication on platforms like Telegram fosters a sense of community and belonging as members rally around shared interests and goals. Here, you can connect with like-minded individuals who share your passion for the crypto space and are eager to collaborate, learn, and grow together. Joining these communities can provide a strong sense of belonging and connection in the often solitary world of cryptocurrency.

Actively participating in crypto communities offers numerous advantages. One of the most significant benefits is access to real-time market sentiment. You can gauge the market's mood by engaging in discussions and monitoring conversations, understanding whether investors are optimistic or cautious. This insight can inform investment decisions, allowing you to respond swiftly to changing conditions. Moreover, these communities provide a platform for peer support and shared learning. As you navigate the complexities of cryptocurrency, having a network of peers to consult can be invaluable. You can share your experiences, learn from others' successes and failures, and collectively troubleshoot challenges that arise along the way.

Selecting the right communities to join requires careful consideration. Look for communities with a healthy size and activity level, often indicating a vibrant and engaged membership. A large, active community can offer a wealth of information and perspectives. Still, it should also be well-moderated to ensure discussions remain constructive and on-topic. Pay attention to the quality of moderation and the expertise of community leaders, as these factors contribute to the overall value and reliability of the information shared. Seek forums and groups where knowledgeable members contribute regularly, offering insights that enhance your understanding and keep you informed.

There are several examples of thriving crypto communities that foster engagement and learning. The BitcoinTalk forums have long been a cornerstone of the crypto community, providing a platform for technical discussions and project announcements. Here, you can delve into detailed conversations about blockchain technology, mining, and market trends. Discord servers dedicated to niche cryptocurrency interests offer another layer of specialized knowledge. These servers often host channels focused on specific topics, allowing you to connect with experts and enthusiasts who share your interests. Whether you're interested in a particular altcoin, blockchain application, or investment strategy, there's likely a Discord community where you can find valuable insights and make meaningful connections.

Attending Webinars and Workshops to Further Your Education

See yourself stepping into a room filled with anticipating minds, tuned into cryptocurrency's nuances. Webinars and workshops offer these vibrant spaces where learning extends beyond reading and into live interaction. These events present unique opportunities for engaging with industry experts who generously share their vast knowledge and experience. You can pose questions in real time during Q&A sessions, gaining clarity on complex topics directly from those at the forefront of the industry. This interactive environment fosters a more in-depth understanding and allows you to connect with others and share interests, expanding your network meaningfully. Such connections can be invaluable, offering insights and fostering collaborations that might not have been possible otherwise.

Finding these valuable events requires a bit of strategy. Platforms like Eventbrite and Meetup are treasure troves for discovering local and virtual events tailored to the crypto enthusiast. You can stay informed about upcoming webinars and workshops by following industry leaders on social media or subscribing to their newsletters. These leaders often host or speak at events, providing firsthand insights into market trends and technological advancements. Keeping an eye on what's happening ensures you won't miss opportunities to learn from the best, whether at a small local gathering or a large international conference.

Continuous education is not just beneficial; it is necessary in the fast-paced world of cryptocurrency. The landscape constantly changes, with new technologies and regulatory updates appearing regularly. Adapting to these changes requires ongoing learning, ensuring you remain informed and agile. Through webinars and workshops, you can stay updated on the latest developments, such as advancements in blockchain technology or shifts in global regulatory frameworks. This commitment to learning empowers you to make informed decisions, enhancing your ability to navigate the crypto market confidently.

Several notable crypto events stand out for their high-quality content and networking opportunities. Consensus by CoinDesk is one such event renowned for bringing together industry leaders, innovators, and investors from around the globe. This conference offers a platform for exploring the latest trends and technologies, providing a comprehensive view of the crypto ecosystem. Similarly, the Crypto Finance Conference is another prominent event, offering insights into the intersection of finance and cryptocurrency. Attending these conferences broadens your knowledge and connects you with a group of like-minded people passionate about shaping the future of finance.

Expanding Your Knowledge Base with Podcasts and Books

Find yourself on a long drive or a morning jog. Instead of tuning into the usual radio chatter, you plug into a world of innovation and insight. In this way, podcasts come into play, offering a seamless way to expand your understanding of cryptocurrency without disrupting your daily routine. "The Pomp Podcast" is a favorite among crypto enthusiasts, hosting interviews with industry leaders and influencers who share their experiences and predictions. Listening to these conversations can feel like being a fly on the wall in a room full of visionaries, offering a unique perspective on the rapid changes in the crypto world. Another gem is "Unchained," where host Laura Shin dives deep into the most pressing crypto community issues, from regulatory challenges to groundbreaking technological advancements. These podcasts keep you informed and inspire new ways of thinking about digital currencies.

Books, with their depth and rigor, provide another layer of understanding that complements the immediacy of podcasts. For those seeking to grasp the foundational concepts of cryptocurrency, "The Bitcoin Standard" by Saifedean Ammous is an essential read. It explores the economic principles that underpin Bitcoin, drawing parallels with historical monetary systems and offering a compelling argument for its future potential. Meanwhile, Andreas M. Antonopoulos's "Mastering Bitcoin" is a must-read for anyone interested in the tech side of Bitcoin and blockchain technology. This book breaks down complex topics into accessible language, and it is a valuable resource for anyone eager to understand the mechanics behind the headlines. Both books offer diverse perspectives, enriching your knowledge and equipping you with the insights to navigate the crypto landscape confidently.

Incorporating diverse media into your learning routine can significantly enhance your understanding of cryptocurrency. Audio content, like podcasts, allows you to learn on the go. Whether you're commuting to work, exercising, or doing household chores, listening to a podcast can turn these moments into opportunities for growth. Conversely, books offer the chance to delve deeper into subjects, providing comprehensive exploration and reflection. You can absorb information differently by engaging with both mediums, reinforcing your knowledge, and staying updated on the latest developments. This multifaceted approach to learning keeps you informed and flexible, ready to seize opportunities as they arise.

Integrating educational content into your daily life doesn't require a complete schedule overhaul. Minor adjustments can make a significant difference. Consider setting aside time each week for dedicated reading, treating it as an appointment with yourself to explore new ideas. This time could be as simple as dedicating your morning coffee time or winding down in the evening with a book. Still, your mind is free, such as during your daily commute or while exercising. By weaving these learning opportunities seamlessly into your routine, you create a continuous stream of knowledge that keeps you engaged and informed.

Tools and Apps to Use for Tracking Your Investments

Managing cryptocurrency investments effectively is similar to tending a flourishing garden; it requires attention, care, and the right tools to ensure growth. In the fast-paced world of crypto, where values can shift dramatically within hours, having a robust system for tracking your portfolio is crucial. Enter portfolio tracking applications—your digital assistants are designed to keep a watchful eye on your investments. Blockfolio is one such app offering real-time portfolio updates that allow you to monitor your assets as they navigate the turbulent market waters. It provides a snapshot of your holdings, tracks value changes, and helps you make informed decisions based on current data. Another invaluable tool is CoinTracker. While it also helps in tracking, its strength lies in tax reporting, offering features that simplify calculating capital gains and losses. Integrating these applications into your investment routine gives you clarity and control over your financial landscape.

Regularly monitoring your investments is not just a best practice; it's necessary in the volatile crypto market. By closely monitoring your portfolio, you can identify performance trends that indicate whether your strategy is yielding the desired results. This insight lets you adjust your approach, buying or selling assets as needed to capitalize on favorable conditions. Moreover, prompt responses to market changes can differ between minor setbacks and significant losses. With the right tools, you can stay ahead of the curve, making timely decisions that protect and grow your investments. The market is a living, breathing entity; regular check-ins ensure you're in tune with its rhythm.

Setting up alerts and notifications is an effective way to stay informed without being overwhelmed. Many tracking apps allow you to configure alerts for specific price thresholds, notifying you the moment an asset reaches your target value. This feature helps execute trades swiftly without constantly staring at a screen. Additionally, news alerts for holdings in your portfolio keep you updated on developments that might affect their value. These notifications allow you to act quickly, whether capitalizing on a sudden surge or mitigating potential losses from adverse news. You maintain a proactive stance by leveraging alerts and are ready to engage with the market on your terms.

Effective tracking strategies go beyond merely observing numbers; they involve structured reviews and assessments. Weekly performance reviews are a practical approach to staying informed about your portfolio's health. This process consists of analyzing changes in asset values, comparing them to market trends, and identifying areas for improvement. It provides a detailed overview, helping you understand the factors driving your portfolio's performance. Additionally, diversification analysis is crucial for managing risk. By evaluating the distribution of assets across different sectors and currencies, you ensure that your portfolio remains balanced and resilient against market fluctuations. This strategic review process empowers you to make informed adjustments, optimizing your investments for long-term success.

Portfolio Management Checklist

To optimize your crypto investment strategy, developing a comprehensive portfolio management checklist is crucial. This list should encapsulate essential tasks that streamline your tracking and decision-making process.

- Start by setting up real-time alerts for price fluctuations and news updates relevant to your investments. Then, review your portfolio weekly to assess performance, adjust strategies, and rebalance assets as needed.

- Diversification analysis is another key task involving evaluating your asset spread to ensure it aligns with your risk tolerance and investment goals. This step helps mitigate risks and enhance the potential for returns by spreading investments across various cryptocurrencies and sectors within the blockchain space.

- Incorporating these practices into a structured routine fosters a disciplined approach to cryptocurrency investing. It empowers you to stay ahead of market trends, make informed decisions, and optimally position your digital assets for growth.

Adhering to this checklist organizes your investment efforts and significantly increases your chances of achieving long-term wealth in the ever-evolving crypto landscape.

Adapting to the Evolving Crypto Landscape to Stay Ahead

In the rapidly shifting world of cryptocurrency, adaptability isn't just an advantage—it's a necessity. The crypto market's dynamic nature demands a flexible mindset and a willingness to embrace change. It's about understanding that what works today might not work tomorrow as new technologies emerge and market conditions evolve. Embracing these changes opens opportunities that can significantly impact your financial growth. For instance, staying attuned to technological and market shifts means recognizing when a strategy needs tweaking or when a new investment avenue presents itself. This flexibility isn't about abandoning your principles but adjusting your sails to effectively harness the winds of change.

Recent trends and innovations have added new dimensions to the crypto landscape, reshaping how we interact with digital assets. Non-fungible tokens (NFTs) have brought the talents of artists, collectors, and investors alike into the crypto space, offering a new and unique way to own and trade digital art and collectibles. Unlike cryptocurrencies like Bitcoin, NFTs are one-of-a-kind assets documenting the ownership of a specific item or content on the blockchain. Their vast applications range from digital art and music to virtual real estate. Meanwhile, cross-chain interoperability solutions are breaking down silos between different blockchain networks, allowing them to communicate and share information seamlessly. This development enhances the functionality and utility of blockchain technology, paving the way for more integrated and versatile applications across various platforms.

Proactive learning and adaptation are key to staying up-to-date and capitalizing on these developments. Regularly revisiting your investment theses ensures they remain aligned with current market realities. This involves critically assessing your assumptions about the market, evaluating whether they still hold, and adjusting as necessary. Engaging with cutting-edge projects is another way to stay at the forefront of innovation. By exploring new ventures and technologies, you expand your knowledge and position yourself to exploit emerging opportunities. This engagement involves participating in beta tests, joining developer communities, or staying informed about the latest advancements in the crypto space.

Numerous examples of individuals and organizations have thrived by adapting to the ever-changing crypto landscape. Consider those who embraced decentralized finance (DeFi) platforms early on. By recognizing the potential of DeFi to democratize financial services, these pioneers positioned themselves for significant gains as the sector grew. Similarly, investors who pivoted their focus in response to regulatory changes avoided potential pitfalls and leveraged new opportunities. This adaptability highlights the importance of staying informed and being ready to adjust your short and long-term strategies based on external factors. It underscores the notion that success in the crypto world often hinges on your ability to navigate its complexities with agility and foresight.

As you continue to engage with the world of cryptocurrency, remember that staying ahead requires more than just keeping up with the latest news—it's about being proactive and open to change. This mindset will serve you well as you explore digital assets' vibrant and ever-evolving landscape. Adaptability ensures you remain resilient in the face of uncertainty and poised to seize opportunities as they arise.

Conclusion

A s we close this journey, let's revisit the key insights and knowledge we've explored throughout this book. We've embarked on a path to understanding the intricate world of cryptocurrency, breaking down complex concepts into digestible, simple terms. From defining cryptocurrency and explaining the workings of the blockchain to exploring the safety and security of digital assets, we've laid the foundation for you to step confidently into the crypto market.

We've navigated the essential tools and strategies for safely buying, storing, and trading cryptocurrency. You now understand the importance of choosing reputable exchanges, securing your digital assets with strong passwords and two-factor authentication, and being vigilant against scams and fraud. We've also delved into trading strategies and risk management, equipping you with the information to make well-informed decisions that match your financial goals.

The key takeaway from our exploration is empowerment. By simplifying these complex topics, I have aimed to give you the confidence to engage securely with cryptocurrencies. Understanding these basics allows you to make knowledgeable decisions and approach this digital frontier with intention and clarity. Remember, cryptocurrency is not just for techies; it is available to anyone willing to learn and adapt.

This guide is designed to unravel the complexities of the cryptocurrency world, making it accessible and understandable for everyone. Embracing a mindset focused on continuous learning and growth is crucial as you embark on this adventure. By basing your financial choices on solid knowledge and understanding, you'll be better equipped to move through the cryptocurrency landscape confidently and securely. It's about transforming what may initially appear as an intimidating array of information into a clear path toward making informed and safe investment decisions. This journey is not just about buying and selling; it's about building a foundation that supports your financial well-being in the digital age.

Embarking on your cryptocurrency journey can be both exciting and daunting. With the foundational knowledge you've gained, you're poised to navigate the crypto world more confidently. The first step could be as simple as purchasing a small amount of Bitcoin to familiarize yourself with the process or dipping your toes into the diverse world of altcoins. Each action you take should be driven by curiosity and caution. Embark on your cryptocurrency journey with diligence and informed decision-making underpinned by meticulous research. The notorious volatility of the cryptocurrency market necessitates a continual awareness of the latest trends, developments, and news to navigate its tumultuous waters effectively. However, it's imperative not to let apprehension deter you from delving into the vast potential digital currencies present for wealth accumulation. Achieving financial growth through cryptocurrencies is possible, but it demands a shrewd and patient strategy. Cultivate a balanced perspective that embraces the opportunities while being acutely aware of and prepared for the inherent risks. Remember, each cryptocurrency should align with your financial goals and risk tolerance. Start small, learn continuously, and gradually expand your portfolio. This way, you can experience the market dynamics without exposing yourself to undue risk. Your journey in cryptocurrency is unique, and with a vigilant, informed, and exploratory attitude, you can navigate it successfully to potentially secure your financial future.

In cryptocurrency's dynamic and ever-evolving landscape, staying informed and continuously learning is not just beneficial; it's essential.

The cryptocurrency world is characterized by rapid changes, with new technologies, coins, and investment opportunities emerging quickly. To navigate this complex environment with confidence and success, engaging actively in ongoing education is crucial. One effective way to stay ahead of the curve is by becoming part of crypto communities. These online forums and social media groups are goldmines of information where enthusiasts, experts, and newcomers share insights, news, and tips. Participating in these communities can provide real-time updates, answer your queries, and expose you to diverse perspectives on the crypto market. Moreover, attending webinars and online courses can significantly enhance your understanding of cryptocurrency. These platforms offer structured learning opportunities from industry experts on various topics, from the basics of blockchain technology to advanced trading strategies. They often include live Q&A sessions, allowing you to directly clarify doubts and interact with seasoned professionals. Exploring further educational resources is another key strategy. This includes reading books, following reputable crypto news websites, and subscribing to newsletters. With a plethora of information available, it's vital to select credible and up-to-date sources to ensure you're getting accurate and relevant information. Committing to continuous learning and leveraging these resources will equip you with the knowledge and skills to make informed decisions. This proactive approach to education will keep you informed about the latest developments and open up new opportunities for investment and growth in cryptocurrency.

I want to express my passion and unwavering commitment to your journey. I aim to help individuals like you achieve financial growth and security through cryptocurrency. Your success in navigating this digital frontier is my utmost priority. I am here to support you every step of the way, ensuring you feel confident and secure in your decisions.

In wrapping up, let's end on a positive note.: Cryptocurrencies have the potential to revolutionize personal finance and reshape the global economy. They present a unique opportunity for innovation, promising a new era of financial freedom and wealth creation. As we stand on the brink of this financial frontier, it's crucial to approach with an open mind and a willingness to explore the vast possibilities. The finance landscape is undergoing a seismic shift, heralding the dawn of a new age. By embracing this change and participating in cryptocurrencies, you position yourself at the forefront of economic transformation. This is an opportunity to witness history in the making and actively contribute to the financial innovations that will define the future.

For more people to benefit from the information in this book, they need your help. If this book was informative and of use to you, please leave an honest review to help others recognize this resource.

Thank You,
George Munson

Glossary

- **Address**: A string of characters representing a destination for cryptocurrency transactions.

- **Altcoin**: Any cryptocurrency other than Bitcoin.

- **Arbitrage**: Buying cryptocurrency on one exchange and selling it on another for a profit due to price differences.

- **ATH (All-Time High)**: The highest price ever reached by a cryptocurrency.

- **Bag Holder**: An individual holding on to a significantly decreased value cryptocurrency.

- **Bear Market**: A market condition characterized by prolonged price declines.

- **Bitcoin (BTC)**: The first and most widely known cryptocurrency, created by Satoshi Nakamoto.

- **Blockchain**: A decentralized digital ledger that records transactions securely and transparently.

- **Bull Market**: A market condition characterized by rising prices and optimism.

- **Burning**: Permanently removing a cryptocurrency from

circulation by sending it to an unrecoverable address.

- **Centralized Exchange (CEX)**: A cryptocurrency exchange managed by a central authority, such as Binance or Coinbase.

- **Cold Wallet**: A cryptocurrency wallet not connected to the internet, used for secure long-term storage.

- **Consensus Mechanism**: The method by which blockchain networks agree on the validity of transactions, such as Proof of Work (PoW) or Proof of Stake (PoS).

- **Cryptography**: The use of mathematical algorithms to secure data, fundamental to blockchain technology.

- **DeFi (Decentralized Finance)**: Financial services built on blockchain networks without intermediaries.

- **DYOR (Do Your Own Research)**: An admonition for investors to conduct independent research before making decisions.

- **FOMO (Fear of Missing Out)**: The fear of missing an investment opportunity, leading to impulsive buying.

- **Fork**: A blockchain protocol change, potentially creating a new cryptocurrency (e.g., Bitcoin Cash).

- **Gas Fees**: Transaction fees paid for processing operations on blockchain networks like Ethereum.

- **Genesis Block**: The first block of a blockchain, starting the network.

- **Hash**: A cryptographic representation of data, used for security and transaction verification.

- **HODL (Hold On for Dear Life)**: a term that encourages

long-term cryptocurrency holding despite market volatility.

- **Hot Wallet**: A cryptocurrency wallet connected to the internet that is suitable for frequent transactions.

- **ICO (Initial Coin Offering)**: A method of raising funds by offering new cryptocurrencies to investors.

- **Immutable**: A feature of blockchain technology that ensures data cannot be altered or deleted once recorded.

- **Liquidity**: The ease with which an asset can be bought or sold in the market without affecting its price.

- **Market Cap (Market Capitalization)**: The total value of a cryptocurrency, calculated by multiplying its current price by the circulating supply.

- **Mining**: The process of validating blockchain transactions and earning cryptocurrency rewards.

- **Moon**: A slang term describing a cryptocurrency experiencing a significant price increase.

- **NFT (Non-Fungible Token)**: A unique digital asset stored on the blockchain, often used for art, music, or collectibles.

- **Node**: A computer that participates in a blockchain network by storing and validating its data.

- **Oracles**: Third-party services that provide off-chain data to smart contracts, enabling them to interact with real-world information.

- **Private Key**: A secret cryptographic key used to access and manage cryptocurrency in a wallet.

- **Proof of Stake (PoS)**: A consensus mechanism where validators are selected based on the amount of cryptocurrency they hold and "stake."

- **Proof of Work (PoW)**: A consensus mechanism that requires miners to solve complex mathematical puzzles to validate transactions.

- **Public Key**: A cryptographic code associated with a private key, used to receive cryptocurrency.

- **Rug Pull**: A scam where developers withdraw funds from a cryptocurrency project and abandon it.

- **Satoshi**: The smallest unit of Bitcoin, equal to 0.00000001 BTC, named after its creator.

- **Smart Contract**: Self-executing programs stored on a blockchain to automatically enforce agreements when predetermined conditions are met.

- **Stablecoin**: A cryptocurrency pegged to a stable asset, such as the US dollar, to reduce volatility (e.g., USDT, USDC).

References

- *95+ Reddit Cryptocurrency & Bitcoin Subreddit - CryptoLinks: Best crypto & Bitcoin sites | Trusted reviews & top resources.* (n.d.). CryptoLinks. https://cryptolinks.com/reddit-cryptocurrency

- Academy, B. (2024, December 14). *What is a crypto wallet and how to choose the right one?* Binance Academy. https://academy.binance.com/en/articles/crypto-wallet-types-explained

- Admin, & Admin. (2024, July 27). *How to avoid common crypto scams.* Crypto Expanse. https://themooningcrypto.com/2024/07/27/how-to-avoid-common-crypto-scams/

- Bajpai, P. (2024, November 16). *What is cryptocurrency cold storage and which method is safest?* Investopedia. https://www.investopedia.com/articles/investing/030515/what-cold-storage-bitcoin.asp

- Baker, W. (2025, March 27). *Best Crypto exchanges and apps for April 2025.* Investopedia. https://www.investopedia.com/best-crypto-exchanges-5071855

- Bisa, T. (2023, August 25). Understanding phishing attacks and how to avoid them. *Secrash - Bug Bounty Tips.*

https://www.secrash.com/search/label/Phishing

- Brooks, M. (2024, December 27). *The 12 best Crypto news websites in 2025.* Coin Ledger, Inc. https://coinledger.io/tools/best-crypto-news-sites

- Cointelegraph. (2024a, August 28). *Crypto charts 101: How to read cryptocurrency charts.* Cointelegraph. https://cointelegraph.com/learn/articles/crypto-charts-101-how -to-read-cryptocurrency-charts#:~:text=The%20top%20of%20t he%20bar,right%20represents%20the%20closing%20price

- Cointelegraph. (2024b, September 18). *A beginner's guide to earning passive income with DeFi.* Cointelegraph. https://cointelegraph.com/learn/articles/decentralized-finance-a -beginners-guide-to-earning-passive-income-with-defi#:~:text=C hoose%20a%20platform%3A%20Commonly%20used,pair%20t o%20the%20liquidity%20pool.

- Cointelegraph. (2024c, November 11). *How to Verify token Legitimacy: A Step-by-Step Guide.* Cointelegraph. https://cointelegraph.com/learn/articles/guide-to-verifying-toke n-legitimacy

- *Crypto Security: Best practices to protect digital assets.* (2024, September 23). Trakx. https://trakx.io/resources/insights/crypto-security/

- *Cryptocurrency webinars and training - BrightTALK.* (n.d.). BrightTALK. https://www.brighttalk.com/topic/cryptocurrency

- *Digital assets | Internal Revenue Service.* (n.d.). https://www.irs.gov/businesses/small-businesses-self-employed/ digital-assets

- *Digital Surge | Crypto Portfolio Diversification.* (n.d.). Digital

Surge Australia. https://digitalsurge.com.au/education/crypto-portfolio-diversifi cation-with-examples/

- ETMarkets.com. (2024, October 9). From skepticism to acceptance: How institutions are embracing cryptocurrencies. *The Economic Times*. https://m.economictimes.com/markets/cryptocurrency/from-sk epticism-to-acceptance-how-institutions-are-embracing-cryptoc urrencies/articleshow/114071521.cms#:~:text=Increased%20ins titutional%20involvement%20has%20improved,appealing%20fo r%20long%2Dterm%20investors

- Fonseca, V., Pacheco, L., & Lobão, J. (2019). Psychological barriers in the cryptocurrency market. *Review of Behavioral Finance, 12*(2), 151–169. https://doi.org/10.1108/rbf-03-2019-0041

- Gratton, P. (2024, November 20). *Trailing Stop/Stop-Loss combo leads to winning trades.* Investopedia. https://www.investopedia.com/articles/trading/08/trailing-stop -loss.asp

- *Markets in Crypto-Assets Regulation (MICA).* (n.d.). https://www.esma.europa.eu/esmas-activities/digital-finance-an d-innovation/markets-crypto-assets-regulation-mica

- PricewaterhouseCoopers. (n.d.). *PWC Global Crypto Regulation Report 2023.* PwC. https://www.pwc.com/gx/en/about/new-ventures/global-crypt o-regulation-report-2023.html

- Satsuk, P. (2025, January 5). *Fiat Currency vs Cryptocurrency: Fiat and Crypto Rivalry.* WLGLOBAL. https://www.wlglobal.solutions/blog/fiat-and-crypto/

- *Top 21 Crypto Twitter Influencers in 2025 – Coinband.* (n.d.). Crypto & Blockchain Marketing Agency – Coinband. https://coinband.io/blog/crypto-twitter-influencers

- Wade, J. (2025, January 15). *Scams, fees, and lost passwords: Avoid the 10 biggest mistakes of new crypto investors.* Investopedia. https://www.investopedia.com/biggest-mistakes-crypto-investors-make-8712112

- Weston, G. (2025, March 17). *Crypto Wallet Security – A Comprehensive guide.* 101 Blockchains. https://101blockchains.com/crypto-wallet-security/

- *What does HODL mean?* (2025, February 26). Public. https://public.com/learn/hodl-meaning

- *What is cryptocurrency and how does it work?* (2018, December 8). /. https://usa.kaspersky.com/resource-center/definitions/what-is-cryptocurrency?srsltid=AfmBOornoxrJOLdaA0SgDpJ2ootEcorH1udy31aFGIayEuL-CGTnmj3z

- *What is Two-factor-Authentication? Its Importance in Crypto Security | Tangem Blog.* (2023, September 26). What Is Two-factor-Authentication? Its Importance in Crypto Security | Tangem Blog. https://tangem.com/en/blog/post/what-is-two-factor-authentication-2fa/

- Zeller, A. (2025, April 4). Top 7 cryptocurrency trends (2025 and Beyond). *Exploding Topics.* https://explodingtopics.com/blog/cryptocurrency-trends

www.ingramcontent.com/pod-product-compliance
Lightning Source LLC
Chambersburg PA
CBHW071429210326
41597CB00020B/3710

9798992377569